Echoes
ECHOING CHRIST

CONTENTS

Welcome	2
All about *Echoes*	2
Overview of a Studysheet	3
Overview of the Resource	4
Support for Leaders	7
Organising the Parish Sessions	7
Introducing *Echoes* in the Parish	8
Leading a Session	10
Pronunciation Guide	12
Leading Session 1	13
Leading Session 2	21
Leading Session 3	29
Leading Session 4	39
Leading Session 5	47
Leading Session 6	53
Leading Session 7	63
Leading Session 8	69
Leading Session 9	75
Leading Session 10	81
Leading Session 11	87
Comments & Evaluation Form	93
Notes	94

Published by CTS · MARYVALE INSTITUTE

Welcome!

This **leader's guide** accompanies the second edition of the resource, Echoes, which contains eleven studysheets, one for each of eleven sessions for the formation of all those who want to help in any way to pass on the faith to others: catechists, parents and parish volunteers.

This leader's guide contains all the information a group leader needs for using Echoes in the parish or deanery. The guidance set out here has been carefully planned to take a leader through every step of setting up the programme of sessions as well as providing what is needed to prepare and run each session.

Each participant must have their own **participant's pack** of eleven studysheets, one for each session, which you read and work from together and on which participants can write their own notes and comments. Here in the leader's guide, as well as a set of the same studysheets, the leader has details of each session, extra notes and all the handouts necessary for the the whole programme. Handouts, artwork and other parts of the Leader's Guide can be found on the CD.

It is hoped that *Echoes* will awaken in all who use it a thirst to know Christ and his Church better, in order to appreciate more fully the wonder of the merciful love of the Trinity, and to desire that this Good News be brought to the ends of the earth.

All about Echoes

Rooted in parish life

This resource has been developed by a catechetical team who are working at, or associated with, Maryvale Institute. Maryvale is an international distance-learning college serving the Church through adult formation in the areas of catechesis, theology and philosophy. The Institute has worked with catechists from every continent for over twenty years and has developed a number of courses, including BAs and MAs for the formation of catechists. *Echoes* has grown out of this broad experience of formation and catechetical work in parishes. The authors have drawn together the content and method of *Echoes* directly from this experience.

The resource follows the main guidelines outlined in the *General Directory for Catechesis* and the purpose of this resource is to provide *foundational catechetical guidelines* for catechists (volunteers, parents and all those willing to help in any way). The sessions are distilled from the experience of dealing with common misunderstandings and are designed to highlight how the Church thinks and works in order to make it easier for catechists to understand, appreciate and hand on what she believes.

You will notice from the titles of the eleven sessions, then, that the subjects do not follow a systematic doctrinal schema. The authors of the resource are committed to the view that catechesis does, of course, need to be both systematic and kerygmatic. But *Echoes* is trying to provide these more basic foundations, without which an effective catechesis cannot be developed.

Rooted in Tradition

The Church uses the term 'Tradition' for the work of the Holy Spirit guarding and drawing out the riches of all that is of Christ and his kingdom. To be involved in catechesis is to enter into that work of the Holy Spirit in the Church, joining the great river of Tradition, of handing on the faith – and of handing oneself and others over, more and more, into Christ. 'Tradition' comes from the Latin, 'traditio', meaning 'hand on'. This resource speaks of the faith, therefore, as something to be 'handed on', stressing that catechesis is concerned with the passing on of the living Tradition.

The notion of 'handing on' the faith also reminds one of the role of the Magisterium of the Church in the work of catechesis since it is by the laying on of *hands* that a bishop is consecrated to be an authentic teacher and interpreter of the Word of God.

Finally, the notion of 'handing on' emphasises that the work of catechesis is inescapably personal: only persons have hands. The faith is handed on only in and through the lives of persons.

Overview of a studysheet

You will see how this 'handing on' takes place and is encouraged in the context of issues and questions typically raised in a parish if you look now at a studysheet of any session. The content of a session consists simply in working one's way through a studysheet.

For every studysheet you will see that :

- *Each session poses a question.* This is a fundamental question that has been found to underlie a host of other typical questions in parish catechesis. For example, many questions and practices concerning the liturgy fall into place when the question, 'What is the Mystery?' (session 9), is answered. Only by understanding how deeply rooted is the Church's thinking concerning divine mystery can one appreciate why Catholic liturgy is as it is and begin to examine how to portray the wonder of that mystery to others.

- *A Scripture quotation immediately follows the title.* This quotation is the basis for the explanations contained in the session or summarises the answer to the question.

- Each session then follows the *angel's invitation to pray*, that is, to begin by entering immediately into direct contact with the Trinity.

- *The first paragraph*, in the first column, is always a summary of what the session is going to include. This helps everyone get an overview from the outset.

- *Each session has key points.* These points are indicated in sub-headings and made explicit in single-sentences at the conclusion of the sections within the session. They are drawn together in a summary at the end of the session. These summary statements follow the idea of the 'in brief' sections of the *Catechism of the Catholic Church*.

- *Numbered dots* on the sheet correspond to a numbered point in the session notes in the leader's guide. They may indicate a handout, an activity, or additional points which can be made by the leader.

- *A summary* of each session is offered, reminding people of what has been covered.

- There is always a short *thematic glossary* of some of the important but more unusual words used by the Church.

- There are suggestions for *further reading* for those who want to follow up points between sessions.

- *The final prayer* is a prayer of thanksgiving or a well-known prayer of the Church that follows the theme of the session.

- *The pictures* of an angel at the beginning and of Our Lady at the end of each session are signs of the method of annunciation and communication of the Word that has inspired this resource. The pictures in each session further illustrate the point of the session and the title of each picture is given in the leader's guide.

Overview of the resource

The eleven sessions, being rooted in both parish life and in Tradition, each have this double aspect to them. What, then, does the whole resource cover?

Session 1 – What is the Good News?
'The truth will make you free' (Jn 8:32)

The focus of the first session is on the privilege of being a catechist, one who 'echoes' both the message and the Person of Christ. It also helps participants to recognise, in a simple way, that everyone's deepest need in life is for the healing and happiness that Jesus Christ can bring.

The issue in parish life addressed here is that many willing helpers are not aware that the Church has been given, and entrusted with, something specific and precious for us to hand on, and have not been used to articulating what the Good News is.

Painting: *Christ, the Word of Life*

Session 2 – Why the Holy Spirit?
'The Holy Spirit, whom the Father will send in my name, he will teach you all things, and bring to your remembrance all that I have said to you.' (Jn 14:26)

This session focuses on the origins of the Church following the Resurrection of Christ and the descent of the Holy Spirit on the apostles at Pentecost. It explains how the Church has understood the handing on of Christ's life in Scripture and Tradition, interpreted by the Magisterium, and it introduces the main source to draw upon for parents and catechists today, the Catechism of the Catholic Church.

The issue in parish life addressed here is that many willing helpers are unaware of the Church's origins and Tradition and many have not seen that the Church has been given, and entrusted with, a perfect and precious treasure for us to hand on.

Painting: *The Finding of Jesus in the Temple*

Session 3 – Why the Church?
'He who hears you, hears me' (Luke 10:16)

In this session the focus is upon the Church as our mother and teacher. It explains how the teaching authority of the Church, the Magisterium, interprets Scripture and Tradition for us and speaks to us in the name of Christ. The session explores this in more detail from documents of the Second Vatican Council and the letters and writings of the Popes and Congregations in Rome.

The issue arising out of the experience of parish catechetics which is addressed here is that the way the universal Church works to form and safeguard doctrine, the ways in which her documents are written, the extent of the Church's communication, are rarely known.

Painting: *St Joseph*

Session 4 – Why the Catechism?
'Father, this is eternal life… that they may know you.' (John 17:3)

This resource holds the *Catechism of the Catholic Church* in high esteem as an extraordinary gift to the Church of today's world and spends the whole of this session explaining how the Catechism works. The session looks at its structure, its purpose, and how to use it for learning and for teaching the faith.

The Catechism is not yet very familiar to people and its wealth and beauty have often been insufficiently appreciated. This resource gently leads people towards a discovery of the catechetical riches of the Catechism.

Painting: *Psalm 23*

Session 5 – Who teaches?
'As the Father sent me so I send you' (Luke 10:16)

The purpose of this session is to focus on the supreme Catechist, God himself. As catechists we are deeply privileged in being able to share in what is essentially a divine work. This session makes clear how much one can rely on God's presence and providence in every catechetical activity.

We rightly think of God as the main subject matter of our catechesis: our teaching is about him. What is easily forgotten amongst parents, catechists and helpers is that the three Persons of the Blessed Trinity are actively present in the mind and heart of the *catechist*, in the work of *catechesis* and in the lives of *those being catechised*.

Painting: *The Sacred Heart of Jesus*

Session 6 – Whose story?
'He interpreted for them all the Scriptures' (John 20:21)

In this session we look at the Catholic Story, the history of salvation, through the time of the Old Testament, the time of Christ and the time of the Church. This is the wonderful story in which we find our true identity. It is a family story of a people to which we belong.

Many know a few fragmented parts of the story of salvation but few people have a sense of the whole, or of its plan or unity. For some even the life story of Christ is not easily recalled. We all need to know the broad brush strokes of the story, which is our heritage by adoption, and be able to tell it to others. It is the context and perspective within which we can place our thoughts and teaching on all other matters.

Painting: *Mother and child reading the word*

Session 7 – Who are we?
'You shall be consecrated to me' (Exodus 22:31)

The question, 'Who are we?' refers to who we are as catechisers, who we are in terms of the mission of the Church. This session explains the Church's mission as Christ's, described from the earliest times as that of the prophet, priest and king. It goes on to explain the lay person's mission in the same terms.

This session tries to clarify some of the frequent misunderstandings that arise with the increase in lay participation, if the complementarity of roles is not well understood. The identity of prophet, priest and king is shared by the clergy and the lay faithful in different but complementary ways, 'for in the Church there is diversity of ministry but unity of mission' (CCC 873).

Painting: *Baptism of Christ*

Session 8 – Why link with the Liturgy?
Christ, our spiritual and eternal sacrifice' (cf. Heb 9:14)

This session explores the links between catechesis and the liturgy. It considers what liturgy is and examines five key elements of liturgy which are important for any catechesis. Finally, it looks at three practical ways of making catechesis liturgical.

This session is to help fulfil the Church's ardent desire 'that all the Christian faithful be brought to that full, conscious and active participation which is required by the very nature of the liturgy and the dignity of the baptismal priesthood' (GDC 85).

Painting: *The presentation of Jesus in the Temple*

Session 9 – What is the Mystery?
'Worship the Father in Spirit and in Truth' (Jn 4:23)

The topic in this session is the Mystery - the plan and design of God for our good, for our salvation, which would have remained unknown had God not chosen to reveal it to us. Through Christ we are given a privileged view into the life of God himself.

This session is to remind people that all catechesis is given essentially to invite us to the Paschal Mystery of Christ's sacrifice on the cross in order to insert us more fully into the divine mystery of Christ's Sonship. The session is specifically to help people appreciate more this mystery in its fullest sacramental form made present for us in the Mass.

Painting: *Crucifixion*

Session 10 – What can we do?
'Do whatever he tells you' (Jn 2:5)

This session is focused upon what the *General Directory for Catechesis* calls the 'pedagogy of God'. We see what implications this has for how we can catechise or help. To know what to do is to do it God's way, as he has taught. This is the first principle.

What one can do is also answered by giving practical guidance about the structuring of catechetical sessions, irrespective of the subject, age group or circumstances of those we are teaching, drawing together the principles and key truths of previous sessions.

Painting: *The finding of Jesus in the temple*

Session 11 – What next?
'Put out into the deep!' (Lk 5:4)

Blessed Pope John Paul II quotes this phrase from St Luke in his encyclical for the third Millennium. He encourages us not to be afraid of the deep and in this final session we explore the different meanings of 'the deep', for example the Holy Father speaks of the deep as the 'deep of prayer', and then *why* we are asked to put out into the deep.

In other words, people need to be sure they have Good News to tell and this session briefly sums up the centrality and aim of evangelisation in all our parish activity, concluding with the famous words of Archbishop Oscar Romero about taking 'the long view' with the things of God.

Painting: *St Michael the Archangel*

Support for leaders

As a leader of *Echoes*, support is offered to you in a number of ways:

Your questions answered

Do you have questions about the content, approach or running of *Echoes*? Are you unsure about something in one of the sessions? Did questions arise in a session which you would like to discuss further?

Email your questions or points to: catechesis@maryvale.ac.uk

Write to: Echoes Support, Maryvale Institute, Old Oscott Hill, Birmingham B44 9AG.
Phone: 0121 360-8118 and ask for Echoes Support.
Website: Your will find helpful information and resources on the Maryvale website: **www.maryvale.ac.uk** Look for the *Echoes* button on the website.

Training Days

Regional training days are organised regularly for parish priests, catechists and anyone interested in leading a group using this resource. If you have not yet been on a training day, do consider this. You will meet others who are using *Echoes* for training in the parish and will be given specific guidance in the use of the materials. Contact Maryvale for details of these. You may also decide that you would like to train additional members of the parish to run Echoes.

The Sower

Maryvale Institute publishes **The Sower**, a quarterly journal for the home, parish and school, to assist those who are handing on the faith to others. This provides articles, worksheets and reviews to assist catechists, teachers and parents. Contact the Circulation Manager, The Sower, at Maryvale Institute for details of how to subscribe.

Materials

For all questions concerning the availablility and distribution of *Echoes* materials contact the Catholic Truth Society, 40-46 Harleyford Road, London SE11 5AY.
Tel: 020 7640 0042. Fax: 020 7640 0046. www.cts-online.org.uk

Organising the parish sessions

How often to meet

Sessions can be held weekly, fortnightly or monthly, depending on the parish. A session lasts approximately one and a half hours. There is a good deal of material provided for each session so that there is always more for people to do at home if they wish. Alternatively, the material provided here can support longer sessions for those who choose to meet during the day, for example, and include a packed lunch. It is a good idea to ask the participants to fill in an evaluation form during the final session. This can be helpful for further training sessions, and it also provides an indication of what the participants would like to know more about for future planning of parish talks or catechesis.

Time of Recollection

At the end of the period of sessions, you may like to hold a time of recollection, or mini-retreat, in your parish for the participants of the course, and include, perhaps, other catechists in the parish or those who are interested in following the sessions next time around.

Books and materials needed

Participants do not need any books in order to undertake this training. Everything they are asked to read is provided in the studysheets and in the photocopiable handouts contained in the leader's guide.

Nonetheless we strongly recommend that single copies of a number of key texts are made available at the sessions. These would form part of the parish library which is available for catechists and helpers to use. Participants can browse through these at the sessions and become familiar with using them.

The books recommended to be available for each session are:

- A Catholic Bible (or different versions of Catholic Bibles)
- A copy of the *Catechism of the Catholic Church*
- The Second Vatican Council Documents. The Conciliar and post-Conciliar documents are gathered in two volumes, edited by Austin Flannery.
- *The General Directory for Catechesis,* from the Congregation of the Clergy
- *Novo Millennio Ineunte* – Pope John Paul II's letter on the Third Millennium
- A selection of encyclicals (see notes on leading session 3 for details)

It is also important to encourage people gradually to buy their own copies of these sources for catechetical work, especially the Scriptures and the Catechism, and to bring them to the sessions rather than always work from the photocopiable handouts. Using the books develops 'hands-on' experience and increases confidence in using the sources of Church teaching. Those who wish to purchase books can do so from the Catholic Truth Society or from the Maryvale Bookshop. Also the Vatican website address can be given for looking up Church documents – www.vatican.va

Certificates

As there is no written work for assessment attached to this resource, certificates produced by the parish can be given on the basis of attendance. A suggested format for this is included on the CD. We recommend that participants be expected to attend at least 80% of the sessions if they wish to gain a certificate.

Introducing Echoes in the Parish

1. Promotion

Before beginning the promotion of *Echoes* training it is worth getting dates and a venue arranged so that the date and venue of the introductory session can be publicised. It is helpful for the promotion of *Echoes* in the parish to begin at least two weeks before the introductory session. Promotion is best undertaken in several ways:

- by means of the parish newsletter
- through posters in the Church and in the school
- by an invitation from the Parish Priest at the end of Masses
- by word of mouth.

It is also valuable to link the promotion of *Echoes* to sacramental programmes, especially appealing to parents, who will then be in a better position to take on their role as primary educators of their children in matters in faith, and to those who help in a variety of different ways.

Note that at this stage the notices are best addressed to 'those who wish to share their Catholic Faith with others' rather than 'catechists' because, at this initial stage, a number of people who could benefit from Echoes may not have enough confidence to put themselves forward for 'catechist training'.

Here we offer some ideas about what you might want to cover on an introductory evening when you explain what *Echoes* is and what is involved in using the resource. It would be good to have participants' packs available at this introductory session for people to buy or to look at.

Outline of introductory evening

1. WHAT *ECHOES* AIMS TO DO
- To explore what it means to hand on the faith
- To teach key principles which are important for the transmission of the faith
- To help you to know where to turn in order to find help when teaching the faith to others
- To consider some different methods and ideas for teaching

Overall, it aims to give you confidence in your teaching through knowing and understanding better *what* the Church wants us to teach and *how* the Church wants us to teach.

For those of you who have been involved in catechetical work for a while the training will give opportunities to reflect on what you are doing, to pray, and to examine the Church's vision for our catechetical work, as well as consolidating some practical teaching points.

2. DIFFERENT LEVELS OF PARTICIPATION
- It will be sufficient to just attend the sessions without further study
- But, for those wanting to study more deeply, further reading will be given.

3. STRUCTURE OF THE PROGRAMME
- There are eleven sessions in the programme.
- The suggested duration of the sessions is one and a half hours.

4. RESOURCES
- Nothing is needed except a participant's pack
- Group copies of books will be available at the sessions.
- There will be the facility to purchase some books if you so wish.

5. CERTIFICATE
A Certificate can be presented to the participants at the end of the course based on attendance (at least 80% will be required – 9 of the eleven sessions).

6. COST
To be determined by the Parish Priest.

7. TIME OF RECOLLECTION
If time allows, when the training programme finishes, we hope to have a time of recollection and prayer together. We will be considering, 'Where we go from here?'

8. ENROLMENT FORM
Those who are interested in participating are asked to complete a simple enrolment form which will help us to plan the practicalities of the training to suit everybody's needs as much as possible.

Leading a session

Echoes follows a fairly unusual approach in that it is based on a group studying a text together. The text is read slowly, out loud, with opportunities at regular intervals to stop and check that everyone is following and understanding it. This process allows for a thorough assimilation of the material at a pace that can be handled, and it encourages structured discussion based on understanding the text. It is important for the leader to read the text of the relevant studysheet carefully beforehand, together with the notes on leading that particular session. There are also normally handouts which need to be photocopied.

Some parts of the text are relatively simple; some of it is more demanding. A conscious decision has been made to introduce the rich thinking of the Church on catechesis which is found in the key documents of the Magisterium. Vocabulary which is less familiar is explained in a glossary at the end of each session. There is always more than enough material for each session. How much of the studysheet the group works through will depend on the particular individuals present and the pace that is suitable for them. Normally, though, you will want to anticipate that an activity or part of the studysheet might be completed by participants at home, between meetings. In some cases you might even decide to spread the reading of a studysheet over two meetings rather than one.

Prepare all you need according to the leader's guide for that session, and prepare the room so that people can sit comfortably - preferably around a table or tables because there will be bibles and other books to refer to and people will normally want to take some notes. Have some spare pens or pencils and paper available.

- It is good to start the *introductory* or first session with a drink and biscuits because this helps to welcome people to something new. After that it is probably better to start promptly and *finish* with a time of socialising, preferably over a cup of tea or coffee and biscuits. All this helps to build the parish community. Alternatively, a day session may well take place after Mass and a cup of tea be a welcome break between the two activities.

- Begin by allowing the group to settle, and find the right session studysheet if you have already handed out the complete participant's pack to those present. Alternatively, you may have decided to hand out only the empty folder from the participant's pack initially and hand out the relevant studysheet at each session. This approach means that participants are not tempted to 'study ahead' and it keeps the art works fresh and new for them.

- Once everyone is ready, begin by reading out the title and the Scripture quotation and then after a short pause begin with the prayer. The prayer could be led by one person or prayed together slowly out loud.

- After the prayer, give the introduction in your own words, or read from the first paragraph, as you choose. This is placed below the prayer on the front of the studysheet. It helps everyone to see what is going to be covered during the session.

- Now you are ready to start work by reading through the studysheet. You will need to have thought about whether it will mainly be you, as leader, reading the text, with selected portions read by others, or whether you would like to read in 'round robin' fashion. To some extent you will discover what is best by trial and error. A few points are worth considering as you think about this point:

- Because you will have prepared before and read the text slowly for yourself, you are in the best position to decide which portions are easier to read and which more difficult. You will want to keep the more difficult sections for yourself or only ask those you know will be confident in reading aloud.

    It is important to read *slowly*, and this is something you may want to say at the outset. A slow reading allows everyone in the group to keep up. If a participant does read too hastily you may want to introduce a pause after a relevant paragraph and either give a summary comment yourself or simply check that the group are following.

    Volunteers might read one subtitled section at a time, or you might decide to ask volunteers to read the quotations (in blue boxes). Those who are a bit hesitant can be encouraged to read as the programme progresses, but discretion is important as some people simply prefer not to or have difficulty in reading aloud.

- Stop at the numbered dots. These are points where there is discussion, or additional points suggested for you to make by way of explanation, or where there is an activity. These moments are particularly important. They are times of discovery, discussion and reflection.

- In addition to stopping at the numbered dots, it is a good idea to stop at the end of each section where there is normally a summary sentence to ensure that everybody understands what has been read, and any questions can be answered.

- As far as possible you will need to make sure that discussion does not go off at a tangent; otherwise there will not be time to cover content of the session. If in-depth discussion results, it can be a good idea to suggest some of the further reading as a means of following the points up in more depth, or make a note of this subject for future parish talks. This will enable you to continue with the session.

- Conclude the session by reading out the summary as a reminder of what has been covered and then end with the final prayer together.

If you are awarding a Certificate to those who complete the sessions, you will need to notice if a person misses a session. You may choose to photocopy the leader's notes for that session, to help the person study the session by him or herself. If you need to keep a note on attendance the best way is either to nominate someone to keep a discreet list or to note down those who were present immediately after the session before forgetting.

Pronunciation guide

It is worth checking and practicing the normal (English) pronunciation of the Latin words before you lead a session if you are unfamiliar with them. The syllable that is stressed is given in capital letters. The pronunciation of some other specialist terms is also given.

WORD	PRONUNCIATION
Catechesis	cat-e-KEEY-sis
Catechetics	cat-e-KET-iks
Catechist	cat-e-KIST
Catechein	cat-e-KINE
Catechesi Tradendae	cat-e-KAY-zee tra-DEN-day
Catechumen	cat-e-KOO-men
Catechumenate	cat-e-KOO-men-ut
Christocentric	krist-o-SEN-trik
Dei Verbum	DAY-ee VERB-um
Dominicae cenae	dom-IN-ik-ay CHAY-nay
Ecclesial	ek-LAYS-ee-ul
Ecumenical	ek-you-MEN-ikul
Encyclical	en-SIK-lik-ul
Evangelii Nuntiandi	ee-van-JAY-lee nun-tzee-AND-ee
Expectatio	ex-pec-TATZ-ee-o
Fidei Depositum	FEE-day de-POS-i-tum
Gaudium et Spes	GOW-dee-um et Spes
Lectionary	LEK-shon-arry
Liturgy	LIT-ur-jee
Lumen Gentium	LOO-men JENTZ-ee-um
Magister	MAJ-ist-air
Magisterium	Maj-ist-EAR-ium
Narratio	na-RATZ-ee-o
Novo Millennio Ineunte	NO-vo mill-EN-ee-o in-ay-UN-tay
Paschal	PAS-kul
Pedagogy	PED-a-godg-ee
Sacrosancto Concilium	SAC-ro-SANC-tum con-CHIL-ee-um
Traditio	tra-DITZ-ee-o

Leading Session 1: What is the Good News?

Preparation

Read through session 1 together with these notes carefully yourself before the session, checking particularly that you understand the activities. Think about which sections you will ask participants to read. Practise the pronunciation of Latin-based words if you are not sure.

Photocopy a sufficient number of the 2 handouts for this session, one for each person participating.

Bring to the session pens, pencils, some paper, a copy of a Bible and a *Catechism of the Catholic Church* (and spare copies of both of these if you have them).

Prepare the room to provide a prayerful and welcoming atmosphere. Get refreshments ready.

At the beginning

Give a brief introduction to the course following the suggestion below.

- Welcome! Let us have a quick look at the list of sessions on the back of the introductory letter. This is in your participant's pack. You can see that the sessions are all based on questions. They may not be typical questions but they are fundamental ones as we shall see. You may want to put the session dates onto this sheet. The sessions will be an hour and a half, with refreshments at the end if you have time to stay.

- During the sessions, there will be various activities that will help us to explore the subjects. These are indicated by dots and passages in blue.

- Prayer is a very important part of the programme. We need to pray together as a group, and also privately, that our efforts will bear fruit.

- Before we start, it will help if we understand that we are involving ourselves in the work of God. Some of the material may be familiar to you, but it is hoped that this resource will help us to see what is important and why and to enable us to be more confident in what we are doing. We are going to look at *how the Church wants us to teach* rather than simply *what* she teaches. We can work more fruitfully together if we know *how* a person thinks as well as *what* they think.

- Please note that the course is open to 'all those who wish to share their Catholic faith with others'. Don't be put off by the use of the word 'catechist' in the session notes. From the explanation of the word 'catechist', you will see that it simply means someone who is passing on the good news of Christ, 'echoing' Christ. This applies to anyone who finds him or herself explaining the Catholic faith, in one-to-one situations, in the family, or in larger, more formal groups.

- Let's start by saying the prayer together from your sheet.

At the session

Pray, then read the *title* followed by the *sentence from Scripture*, or ask different people to read these each week.

Then read the introductory paragraph or summarise it in your own words to introduce the session.

Read each subtitled section at a time or ask people in the group to take it in turns stopping at each sentence in bold to make sure people have understood and have the opportunity to make a comment if they want to.

Stop at the numbered dots

❶ This passage from the Gospel of St Matthew is very short and is a powerful one in its simplicity.

After people have made their initial comments you may want to consolidate what they have said by inviting them to look at the *verbs* in the passage:

entered – Jesus enters into our lives, he comes to us where we are

saw – Jesus sees us, he knows us through and through, knows our hopes and aspirations

lying – he knows our condition, prone, helpless, waiting for grace, for help

touched – Jesus engages with us personally, unites himself to us, does not stay aloof

left – the healing is complete; the fever goes; Jesus' grace completely heals us, mends our nature, restores us

rose – the same word, in Greek, as is used for the resurrection. We are healed and live by the power of Christ's resurrection and look forward to our everlasting life and our final healing in heaven

served – Peter's mother-in-law responds beautifully and appropriately, making herself available to him, to do his will and his work.

❷ Explain that this is a famous passage from St Paul, one of the greatest saints of the Church, recognising his own conflicts and need for Christ's grace. The Church teaches that only through grace can we come into the harmony God wants for us. We cannot achieve this by our own efforts, although we must cooperate with God's grace.

Help participants to appreciate the sense of conflict that Paul experienced and gently invite a little exploration of this as a lived reality for members of the group. We can know what is right and want what is good but cannot always manage to do it.

If participants wonder about the meaning of the word 'flesh' in this extract you can explain that this is Paul's way of speaking about the whole of his life that is not in obedience to God, that has not yet come under the sway of grace. It is not particularly a reference to his body, to his physical life.

When the brief discussion has finished, round off this activity by saying the short prayer together.

Come back together for a short question time about anything that is not understood, or other comments.

Read the summary to sum up the session.

Point out that the **further reading** is optional.

Say together the final prayer.

'I do not understand my own actions.

For I do not do what I want, but I do the very thing I hate.

Now if I do what I do not want, I agree that the law is good. So then it is no longer I that do it, but sin which dwells within me. For I know that nothing good dwells within me, that is, in my flesh.

I can will what is right, but I cannot do it.

For I do not the good I want, but the evil I do not want is what I do.

Now if I do what I do not want, it is no longer I that do it, but sin which dwells within me.

So I find it to be a law that when I want to do right, evil lies close at hand. For I delight in the law of God, in my inmost self, but I see in my members another law at war with the law of my mind and making me captive to the law of sin which dwells within my members.'

St Paul, Letter to the Romans 7:15-23

Echoes
Session 1
Handout 2

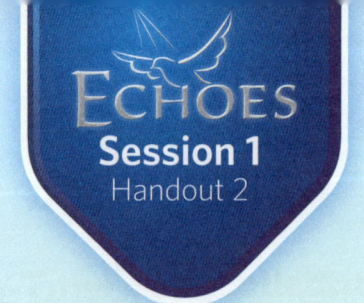

'And when Jesus entered Peter's house,
he saw his mother-in-law lying sick with a fever;
he touched her hand
and the fever left her,
and she rose and served him.'

Matthew 8:14-15

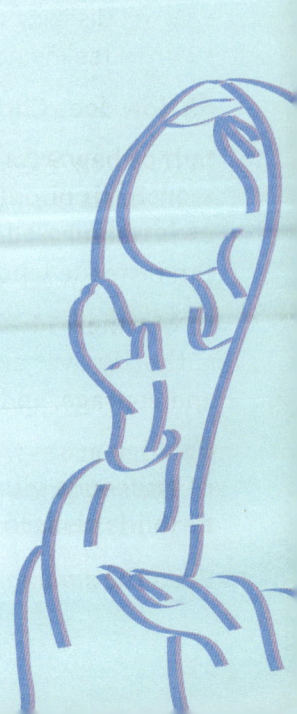

Session 1

What is the Good News?

'The truth will make you free' (Jn 8:32)

*Loving God,
Pour out your Spirit on this parish and grant us a new vision of your glory, a new experience of your power, a new faithfulness to your Word, and a new consecration to your service that your love may grow among us, and your Kingdom come. Amen*

We begin this session by exploring what we mean by the 'Good News' that Christ came to bring. We seek to understand this Good News so that we can pass it on to others.

We then go on to look at the meaning of the title of the course, 'Echoes, Echoing Christ' as a way of understanding who we are as Catholics and what it means to pass on, or 'echo on' the faith of the Church.

Good News

The world in which we wake and live each day appears to us as a puzzle. It is a place of pain, and also of deep happiness. We experience periods of satisfaction, but all too often these are unstable or the satisfaction turns to boredom. We know the promise that love brings but also the numbness that comes with the loss of love or a loved one. The world is a place bright with beauty and hope, but at the same time is filled with dark shadows of injustice, evil and death in which thousands die each day from malnutrition and millions live in loneliness.

The Christian stands in this world able to speak the pure, life-giving words of the Gospel. 'Gospel' means 'Good News'. The Old English word 'gospel' comes from the Anglo Saxon 'godspell' meaning 'good speech or message'. It directly translates the Greek word *'evangelion'* meaning 'Good News'. The Christian can speak this Good News with certainty because it comes with the authority of the God who created the universe and holds it in his hands day by day.

The world has need of this Good News, although it is not always welcome. For like a doctor examining a wound in order to cleanse and heal it, God reveals to us our true condition so that we can seek the only treatment for our healing.

The Diagnosis

The diagnosis: we live in a state of fatal disharmony. The four essential relationships in our lives have received a death-wound. Each of us is in relation with

- God our Creator and Father
- other human beings
- the earth that is our dwelling-place
- our own self that should be a harmonious unity of body, emotions, mind, will and spirit.

The first chapters of the Bible vividly describe the breakdown in these relationships, as disharmony and conflict replace the happiness and stability God seeks for our lives.

The root problem is the mistrust and fear of our very source of life, God the Father, who wants only good for his children. The human person is frightened of a distorted image of the Father who, he thinks, gives him commands and orders obedience, but does not give him what he needs for his happiness. What he thinks God will not give, man then seeks to take for himself. He shuts God out and even treats eternal Love as an enemy.

But cut off from true Life, the human person is like a branch that withers from lack of sap running through it. What he hopes will be a garden of his own making often becomes only a wilderness. Love and true happiness seem to evade so many who are around us. Life is distorted and even destroyed in a vain attempt to secure a good future. Other human beings, the earth, one's bodily life, are ransacked in the search for a final happiness they can never give. When this happens, those around us are used rather than loved, the earth is exploited, the body scarred.

The inner conflict that we all find in ourselves is summed up well by St. Paul in his *Letter to the Romans* 7:14-28.

1 **Look at the passage from Romans Chapter 7 on the handout.**

- **Quietly reflect on the following prayer of the Church: 'Lord, guide us in your gentle mercy, for left to ourselves we cannot do your will.' (Roman Missal, Mass of the Saturday of the Fourth Week of Lent, Opening Prayer).**

The world is in need of healing from all disharmony and distorted relationships.

The Remedy

God reveals our state of sin and ruin to us only gradually. When he comes Jesus says, 'I have many things to say to you, but you cannot bear them now' (Jn 16:12). He lets us see our true condition only as he reveals his plan of loving-kindness, his plan to rescue us. It is not easy to welcome his rescue because it is not easy to face the reality of what our lives become without God. But as our eyes are opened to the immensity of God the Father's love we can gradually accept the truth about ourselves.

To demonstrate his love, the Father sent his Son among us, to lift us out of the pit into which we had fallen. He came to mend our wounded state, to heal our broken relationships and to unite us to the only Source of true life, his Son.

The name given to the remedy is 'redemption', and the simple means by which this is given is 'Baptism', an immersion in water that is made in the name of the Father who made us, the Son who redeems us and the Spirit who guides us into all truth as he renews us.

To live this life of gradual healing in God, we take up our Cross to follow Jesus Christ, who called himself the Way, the Truth, and the Life (Jn 14:6).

Because of the ongoing effects of the state from which we are rescued in Baptism, the state that the Church calls 'original sin', our actions and motives are not automatically good and pure. It is like trying to drive straight with a flat front tyre - you are pulled off the centre of the road, and keeping on course needs a sustained pull on the steering wheel. So it is with our life in Christ: it means holding one's gaze fixed on Christ who is our hope and relying on his grace at every moment.

The Good News is that God the loving Father does not leave us on our own. He sends his Holy Spirit who strengthens us to live in Christ more and more fully. God freely pours out his grace upon us, pours out his own life, to transform each of us into the image of Jesus Christ. 'Grace is everything God grants us, without our deserving it in the least.' (YOUCAT 338).

This is the Good News that each Christian has to share. Not just a message but a new life. Not just a more satisfying life, but the promise of deep joy. This is what we are called to pass on to others. And the name given to the handing on of the Good News is 'catechesis'.

2 **Look up the Gospel account on the Handout of the healing of Peter's mother-in-law by Jesus in Matthew 8:14-15.**

- **Look at the actions of Jesus and of Peter's mother-in-law. What does this tell us about God's work and about our needs and our response to God?**

God has sent his Son and Spirit among us to rescue and heal us.

Catechesis

'Catechesis' is an unfamiliar word to most of us. It comes from the Greek word *catechein*, originally meaning 'to echo'. In the time of St. Paul it was used to mean 'to hear', 'to learn', or 'to instruct'.

Catechesis, then, is about hearing, learning and teaching. And this teaching and learning can be thought of as a kind of echoing. An echo is like a reflection. When we look at a reflection in a mirror we know that what we are looking at is a picture, an image, and not the whole of the reality itself.

A catechist is like a mirror. Those who are learning from a catechist are catching glimpses of a Figure, they are hearing echoes of a Voice who is calling to them and drawing them to Himself through the words and life of the catechist.

The glossary at the end of this session explains the variety of words associated with 'catechesis'.

Echoing a message

Catechesis, then, is the 'echoing' or 'resounding' of a message. It is handing on what has been received. That is what St Paul meant when he said that 'I handed on to you that which was handed on to me' (1 Cor 15:3). St Paul has received the message and now he is 'echoing' it on to others. To be a catechist is to receive and to hand on what has been received.

Catechists hand on a precious message, the Good News. Nothing is more valuable than this, nothing is more important; it is the pearl of great price about which Jesus spoke in the Gospels. It is the News which every person needs to hear.

A catechist, therefore, is one who, realising 'the riches of grace' (Ephesians 1:7) which have been poured out on the world through Christ, is willing to spend time learning about this message of Good News and learning how to teach it so that it may be faithfully and accurately 'echoed' to others.

Scripture calls this precious message a 'Deposit' because it has been entrusted by God to his Church: 'Guard the deposit which has been entrusted to you.' (1 Timothy 6:20). The 'deposit', the riches of Christ's message, have been entrusted to the Church and we all receive this from the Church. We receive it from the Church whose members have, down through the centuries, guarded it, celebrated it, lived it, been nourished by it, and died for it.

Catechesis is an echoing or transmission of a message which the catechist receives from the Church.

Echoing a Person

What we echo is more than just a precious message. We echo a Person. We are not only learning a series of truths and helping others to learn these. We are not only learning *about* Christ. We want to 'gain Christ and be found in Him' (Philippians 3:8-9) and to help others to know and experience the depths of His love. We are opening ourselves, then, to listen not just to a message but to the voice of a Person, the divine Person of Jesus Christ. We are learning to echo Him. In our being with others we are asking others to listen to Him.

The Church teaches that God has said all that He wants to say by sending Christ. Jesus is the Word of God. He is the perfect revelation of God and of His plan of love and salvation. The Father has only one thing He wants to say: 'Listen to my beloved Son, listen to my Word'.

Catechesis is concerned with teaching the faith in order to open the heart to conversion, so that those whom we teach may hear and receive Christ, the Word.

Catechists echo not just a message but a Person.

Summary

In this first session we have been looking at:

- **What is the Good News that we bring?**
- **Our fallen state and how we have been rescued.**
- **What a catechist is.**
- **The catechist as one who echoes both a message and a Person.**

Further reading

- On our original state and the Fall after our first sin: Genesis Chs 1-3; CCC 374, 379; CCC 385-388. *(CCC 374 means Catechism of the Catholic Church, paragraph 374)*
- On the Incarnation of the Son of God: Jn 1:1-18; CCC 456-460.
- On the meaning of the word 'catechesis': CCC 4.
- On proclaiming Christ: CCC 74.

Glossary

Meanings of words associated with catechesis
Catechist: *the person* communicating the message
Catechesis: the *action* of communicating the message
Catechism: a book of the **content** of the message to be communicated
Catechumen: *a receiver* of what is communicated in preparation for Baptism
Catechumenate: the *period* of instruction to catechumens
Catechetics: *guidelines* for communicating

Final meditation and prayer

God has created me to do him some definite service. He has committed some work to me which He has not committed to another.
(John Henry Newman)

Father, let the gift of your life continue to grow in us drawing us from death to faith, hope and love.
Keep us alive in Christ Jesus.
Keep us watchful in prayer and true to his teaching till your glory is revealed in us. Amen.
(Roman Missal: Mass of the 16th Sunday in Ordinary Time, Alternative Opening Prayer)

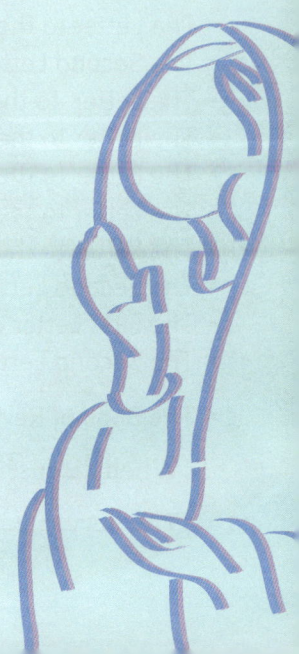

Leading Session 2: Why the Holy Spirit?

Preparation

Read through session 2 carefully yourself, together with these notes, before the session, checking particularly that you understand the activities. Think about which sections you will ask participants to read. Practise the pronunciation of Latin-based words if you are not sure.

Photocopy a sufficient number of the 2 handouts for this session so that there is one for each person participating.

Bring to the session pens, pencils, some paper, a copy of the Bible and a *Catechism of the Catholic Church*.

Prepare the room to provide a prayerful and welcoming atmosphere. Get refreshments ready.

At the session

Read out the title and Scripture quotation then say the prayer together.

Read the introductory paragraph or summarise it in your own words.

Read each subtitled section at a time or ask people in the group to take it in turns stopping at each sentence in bold to make sure people have understood and have the opportunity to make a comment if they want to.

Stop at the Numbered dots

❶ Read the activity which is given in blue. It is best to use a bible for this exercise, or copy the list below and point out the four types of writings:

- the Gospels – about the life of Christ
- the Acts – about the life of the Apostles in the early Church including St Paul
- the Letters – some are letters to a church, others are letters from a person
- the Book of Revelation – a mystical account by St John the Evangelist

- The Gospel of Matthew
- The Gospel of Mark
- The Gospel of Luke
- The Gospel of John

- The Acts of the Apostles

- The Letter to the Romans
- The Letter to the Corinthians
- The Second Letter to the Corinthians
- The Letter to the Galatians
- The Letter to the Ephesians
- The Letter to the Philippians
- The Letter to the Colossians
- The Letter to the Thessalonians
- The Second Letter to the Thessalonians
- The First Letter of Paul to Timothy
- The Second Letter of Paul to Timothy
- The Letter of Paul to Titus
- The Letter of Paul to Philemon
- The Letter to the Hebrews
- The Letter of James
- The First Letter of Peter
- The Second Letter of Peter
- The First Letter of John
- The Second Letter of John
- The Third Letter of John
- The Letter of Jude

- The Book of Revelation

   When discussing the Bible, point out that there are different versions – for example,

   The Jerusalem Bible, which is currently used at Mass, and the New Jerusalem Bible. The Revised

Standard Version (RSV) is generally preferred by scholars as the most accurate of all translations and there is now a New Revised Standard Version (NRSV).

You may want to explain that Catholic bibles have a few extra sections in them. These are writings from the Old Testament which were used by St Paul, for example, in his letters and by the whole Church until the 16th century. At that point the protestant leaders chose to use only those parts of the Old Testament which the Jews also accepted as their Scriptures. Some sections of the Old Testament that had been accepted until then by Christians were then removed from protestant bibles.

❷ Read the activity text which is given in blue and then give out the first handout. You might like to begin by reading the shortest quotation, from **2 Thessalonians**. Here you have a reference to Tradition. Participants may also notice the reference to teaching being given 'by letter.' This is a reference to the Scriptures. There is also a strong sense of apostolic authority in the quotation, and so participants may see the Magisterium here, the teaching authority of the Church.

After this, select one more quotation and look for where at least two of the three, appear together, Scripture, Tradition or Magisterium. You may want to suggest that participants complete this activity at home.

❸ Mention that you will be spending a whole session looking at how to use the Catechism in learning about the faith and in teaching the faith. The *Catechism of the Catholic Church* is also a good way of assessing other resources you may have. This is sometimes called the 'new Catechism' because the first universal catechism, simplified into the Penny catechism (which some may remember) was used until the twentieth century. One of the values of the Catechism is that one can see there what the Church considers important to mention. When reading other books on a topic one can check them against the Catechism to see what the book has chosen to include and what it has chosen to leave out. The Catechism is a good gauge for finding a good resource.

❹ Give out handout 2. Read the first two paragraphs together and then look at the questions under no.1. Repeat for numbers 2 and 3.

The answers for handout 2

- **The Mission of the Church:** to guard the deposit of faith.
- **The task given to the Second Vatican Council:** to guard and present better the precious deposit of Christian doctrine, in order to make it more accessible to the Christian faithful and to all people of good will.
- **How did the Council set out to achieve it?** It strived calmly to show the strength and beauty of the doctrine of the faith.
- **What happened twenty years after the Council?** Pope John Paul II convoked an extraordinary assembly of the Synod of Bishops for the 20th anniversary of the close of the Council.
- **What was requested?** The writing of a catechism or compendium of all Catholic doctrine regarding both faith and morals.
- **The Living Sources of faith:** Sacred Scripture, the living Tradition in the Church and the authentic Magisterium, as well as the spiritual writings of the Fathers, Doctors and saints of the Church.

At the end of this activity, if there is only one catechism in the group you might show the members of the group the different sections in the index of citations. It is even better if participants have their own copy to look at and spend a little time becoming familiar with this index.

Come back together for a short question time about anything that is not understood, or other comments.

Read the summary to sum up the session.

Point out that the **further reading** is optional.

Say together the final prayer.

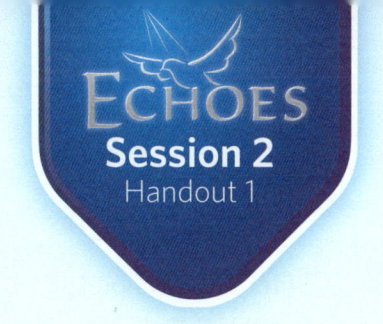

Scripture, Tradition, Magisterium

"He said 'All authority in heaven and on earth has been given to me. Go therefore, make disciples of all nations; baptise them in the name of the Father and of the Son and of the Holy Spirit, and teach them to observe all the commands I gave you. And look, I am with you always; yes, to the end of time."

Matthew 28:18-20

"These remained faithful to the teaching of the apostles, to the brotherhood, to the breaking of bread and to the prayers."

Acts 2:42

"I want to make quite clear to you, brothers, what the message of the gospel that I preached to you is; you accepted it and took your stand on it, and you are saved by it, if you keep to the message I preached to you; otherwise your coming to believe was in vain. The tradition I handed on to you in the first place, a tradition which I had myself received, was that Christ died for our sins, in accordance with the scriptures, and that he was buried; and that on the third day, he was raised to life, in accordance with the scriptures".

1 Corinthians 15:1-4

"Stand firm, then, brothers, and keep the traditions that we taught you, whether by word of mouth or by letter."

2 Thessalonians 2:15

"You must keep to what you have been taught and know to be true; remember who your teachers were, and how, ever since you were a child, you have known the holy scriptures – from these you can learn the wisdom that leads to salvation in Christ Jesus. All scripture is inspired by God and useful for refuting error, for guiding people's lives and teaching them to be upright. This is how someone who is dedicated to God becomes fully equipped and ready for any good work."

2 Timothy 3:14-17

"The president has to be irreproachable since he is God's representative: never arrogant or hot-tempered, nor a heavy drinker or violent, nor avaricious; but hospitable and a lover of goodness; sensible, upright, devout and self-controlled, and he must have a firm grasp of the unchanging message of the tradition, so that he can be counted on both for giving encouragement in sound doctrine and for refuting those who argue against it."

Titus 1:7-9

The Purpose of the Catechism

To my Venerable Brother Cardinals, Patriarchs, Archbishops, Bishops, Priests, Deacons and to all the People of God.

GUARDING THE DEPOSIT OF FAITH IS THE MISSION WHICH THE LORD ENTRUSTED TO HIS CHURCH, and which she fulfils in every age. The Second Vatican Ecumenical Council, which was opened 30 years ago by my predecessor Pope John XXIII, of happy memory, had as its intention and purpose to highlight the Church's apostolic and pastoral mission and by making the truth of the Gospel shine forth to lead all people to seek and receive Christ's love which surpasses all knowledge (cf. Eph 3:19).

The principal task entrusted to the Council by Pope John XXIII was to guard and present better the precious deposit of Christian doctrine in order to make it more accessible to the Christian faithful and to all people of good will. For this reason the Council was not first of all to condemn the errors of the time, but above all to strive calmly to show the strength and beauty of the doctrine of the faith. "Illumined by the light of this Council," the Pope said, "the Church . . . will become greater in spiritual riches and gaining the strength of new energies therefrom, she will look to the future without fear... Our duty is to dedicate ourselves with an earnest will and without fear to that work which our era demands of us, thus pursuing the path which the Church has followed for 20 centuries."

With the help of God, the Council Fathers in four years of work were able to produce a considerable number of doctrinal statements and pastoral norms which were presented to the whole Church. There the Pastors and Christian faithful find directives for that "renewal of thought, action, practices, and moral virtue, of joy and hope, which was the very purpose of the Council."

After its conclusion, the Council did not cease to inspire the Church's life. In 1985 I was able to assert, "For me, then—who had the special grace of participating in it and actively collaborating in its development—Vatican II has always been, and especially during these years of my Pontificate, the constant reference point of my every pastoral action, in the conscious commitment to implement its directives concretely and faithfully at the level of each Church and the whole Church."

In this spirit, on January 25, 1985, I convoked an extraordinary assembly of the Synod of Bishops for the 20th anniversary of the close of the Council. The purpose of this assembly was to celebrate the graces and spiritual fruits of Vatican II, to study its teaching in greater depth in order that all the Christian faithful might better adhere to it and to promote knowledge and application of it.

On that occasion the Synod Fathers stated: "Very many have expressed the desire that a catechism or compendium of all catholic doctrine regarding both faith and morals be composed, that it might be, as it were, a point of reference for the catechisms or compendiums that are prepared in various regions. The presentation of doctrine must be biblical and liturgical. It must be sound doctrine suited to the present life of Christians." After the Synod ended, I made this desire my own, considering it as "fully responding to a real need of the universal Church and of the particular Churches."

For this reason we thank the Lord wholeheartedly on this day when we can offer the entire Church this "reference text" entitled the *Catechism of the Catholic Church* for a catechesis renewed at the living sources of the faith!

Following the renewal of the Liturgy and the new codification of the canon law of the Latin Church and that of the Oriental Catholic Churches, this catechism will make a very important contribution to that work of renewing the whole life of the Church, as desired and begun by the Second Vatican Council.

Session 2

Why the Holy Spirit?

'The Holy Spirit, whom the Father will send in my name, he will teach you all things, and bring to your remembrance all that I have said to you.' (Jn 14:26)

Come Holy Spirit, Creator come, from thy bright heavenly throne. Come take possession of our souls and make them all thine own. O guide our minds with thy blest light, with love our hearts inflame, and with your strength which never decays confirm our mortal frame. Amen

In session one we deepened our understanding of Jesus Christ as 'Good News'. Jesus is Good News because he is the Redeemer of the world. Our world is damaged, wounded and needs healing. This session explores how the Holy Spirit works in the Church to make this Good News known to the world.

Three key terms are introduced in this session: Tradition, Scripture and Magisterium. The Holy Spirit hands on Christ in and through the Church's Living Tradition and her Scriptures, and the voice of Christ also speaks to the world today through her Magisterium. Let us see what this means.

Pentecost

First, let us remember Pentecost. Let us remember what happened fifty days after the Resurrection of Jesus from the dead. Look again at the Scripture passage from John's Gospel at the beginning of this session.

Notice that the three persons of the Trinity are all mentioned. The apostles gathered in an upper room; Jesus' promise came true; the apostles were filled with the Holy Spirit; it was the moment the Church was born.

John's Gospel tells us many things to answer the question 'Why the Holy Spirit?' - that is, why the Apostles needed the Holy Spirit, and what the Holy Spirit would do for them. Already in the quotation for this session we see that the Holy Spirit will *'teach them* all things' and will *'bring to their remembrance'* all that Christ had said to them. In another passage John tells us that the Holy Spirit will *'guide them* into all the truth' (Jn 16:13).

The Holy Spirit is the sure teacher, reminder and guide for the Apostles as they lead Christ's disciples in the early Church.

Handing on Christ

The Church 'hands on' Christ. In the Gospel of Matthew Jesus explains to his disciples what this means when he says,

'Go therefore and make disciples of all nations, baptising them in the name of the Father, and of the Son and of the Holy Spirit, teaching them to observe all that I have commanded you' (Matt 28:19-20).

'Handing on' Christ, then, means going to people and telling them about Jesus Christ so that they can be disciples (a word which means 'followers'). Jesus' disciples are those who listen and learn from him and who go where he goes, who think as he thinks, who love what he loves and who pray to him. The Church also 'hands on' Christ when she baptises and when she celebrates the other sacraments. And she teaches her members how to live in Christ by 'observing' all that he 'commanded' and taught.

The Latin for 'handing on' or 'handing over' is 'Traditio', from which we get the word **Tradition**. Notice that Tradition, the handing on of Christ, was taking place before anything was written down in the New Testament and has continued everyday wherever the Church lives. It is the work of the Holy Spirit in the Church. It includes the teaching of the apostles, celebrating the sacraments, praying and living in Christ.

Magisterium

The apostles appointed successors to continue to their work, called 'bishops' (which means 'overseers'). The successors of the Apostles are the 'masters' or 'master teachers' of the Truth and of what Jesus truly said, and they are guided continually by the Holy Spirit. The Latin word for 'master' is *magister*, from which we derive the word **Magisterium**. The bishops in union with the successor of Peter, the bishop of Rome, are the magisterium and we can trust that the Holy Spirit keeps his promises to them. Reading the writings of the magisterium, then, is a way of knowing with certainty that the words of Jesus are being remembered and interpreted truly for us today.

In the Tradition of the Church guided by the Magisterium we meet the living body of Christ. In this way, the Holy Spirit hands on Christ, from generation to generation.

The Bible

Where does the Bible fit in? The churches founded by the apostles were teaching, listening, believing, baptising, celebrating the Eucharist, and living Christian lives for many years before any writings about Christ were gathered together into what we now know as the New Testament.

The first Christians were also reflecting deeply upon God's deeds and promises in the Old Testament, rejoicing in all that had now been fulfilled in Christ. They knew that these Scriptures were written under the inspiration of the Holy Spirit and have God as their divine author. This is why the Catechism of the Catholic Church says about both the Old and New Testaments:

'Through all the words of Sacred Scripture, God speaks only one single Word, his one utterance in whom he expresses himself completely' (CCC 102).

When the authors of the four Gospels began to preserve in writing the truth of what Jesus said and did, who he was and what happened to him, they were able to include how the Old Testament also spoke of Christ as the One who fulfilled the promises of God.

1 **Look at the structure and contents of the New Testament. Notice the letters and who they are from. Then identify the four Gospels, then the Acts of the Apostles, then finally the Book of Revelation.**

The Bible is a single book and at the same time a library. It is made up of different writings born over a thousand year period. The writings tell of many different figures, they have different human authors, they are written in a variety of literary styles and they have emerged from different historical contexts. But there is a single God revealing Himself through them, and they tell of a single plan of salvation that unfolds in history. Moreover, the writings are directed to a single People of God. And, finally, they have a common centre in Christ. Every page of the Scriptures can be properly understood only in the light of this single plan of salvation and by reference to Christ.

Note on finding Bible references

The Bible is divided into books, chapters and verses. A Bible reference tells us which book, chapter and verse we should go to in order to find the lines we want. The books of the Bible are given in abbreviated form. So, for example 'Rom 1:20' means St Paul's Letter to the Romans, Chapter 1 and verse twenty.

2 **Let us look at some verses from the New Testament. Find and read the following portions from the Scriptures and see whether you can identify any of the three elements of Tradition, Magisterium and Scripture.**

- **Matthew 28:18-20**
- **Acts of the Apostles 2:42**
- **1 Corinthians 15:1-4**
- **2 Thessalonians 2:15**
- **2 Timothy 3:14-17**
- **Titus 1:7-9**

When we want to hand on Christ we need to be nourished by the Scriptures.

Already from the New Testament writers of the early Church one can identify the living message of salvation which was being carefully taught, received, delivered, held and passed on.

God reveals Himself and His single plan of salvation to us in Scripture and Tradition. These are the living wells from which we drink so as to be able to quench our own and others' thirst for the living Lord.

We look to Scripture *and* Tradition, guided by the Holy Spirit promised to the Magisterium, *in order to receive and hand on the true life and message of Jesus Christ.*

The Catechism of the Catholic Church

The Catechism of the Catholic Church is a wonderful example of Scripture and Tradition gathered together by the Magisterium for our day. It was finalised in 1997, and is a completely up-to-date account of the Catholic faith. Every Catholic adult should have a copy on his or her bookshelf. We can turn to this reference work when we would like to know and understand the teaching of the Church on any subject.

We conclude today's session by looking at the introduction to the Catechism, written by Blessed Pope John Paul II. This introduction is called *'Fidei Depositum'*, the Deposit of Faith. This is a phrase used by St Paul for the 'treasure' that has been given, or 'deposited' for safe keeping for all generations, to the Church by God the Father. The treasure is God the Son and the Holy Spirit, who are the treasure of the truth about life and happiness. This is the treasure of the faith of the Church.

Catechism

1. Read the opening two paragraphs of *'Fidei Depositum'* and find:
   - how the mission of the Church is described.
   - the task given to the Second Vatican Council by Pope John XXIII,
   - how the Council set out to achieve this task.

2. Read the paragraphs down to the next main heading.
   - What happened 20 years after the Council? What was requested?

3. Notice that the Catechism will provide renewal through connecting its readers to 'the living sources of the faith'. The texts cited in the Catechism are the sources – made 'living' by the Holy Spirit and from which the writers drew inspiration.
   - What are these living sources at the core of the 'deposit of faith'? Check for yourself the index of citations at the back of the Catechism. There you will find Scripture and Tradition.

What did you find when you investigated the index of citations at the end of the Catechism?

Did you see that Scripture is placed first and counts for over half of the whole index? That shows us the vital role that the Scriptures play in providing the foundations for the Church's catechetical work. Then did you see the Creeds, the professions of faith, together with documents from the Church's Councils down through the centuries? Then there were papal writings, references to the law of the Church and to the liturgy, and then to the writings of the Fathers and saints of the Church.

In his introduction to the Catechism the Pope describes this as similar to listening to a great 'symphony' of voices. In the Catechism we hear the voices of the Church down through the centuries coming together in a tremendously inspiring and uplifting harmony. This is the harmony which we as Catholics are called to echo by our lives.

Summary

In this session we have been looking at:

- **The origin of the Church at Pentecost.**
- **The passing on of Christ's life in Scripture and Tradition, guided and protected by the Magisterium.**
- **The Catechism of the Catholic Church as a wonderful example of Scripture, Tradition and magisterium together.**

Further reading

If you have time before the next session you might also like to read the rest of 'Fidei Depositum'.

Final prayer

Come, Holy Spirit, come!
And from your celestial home
Shed a ray of light divine!

You, of comforters the best;
You, the soul's most welcome guest;
Sweet refreshment here below;

In our labour, rest most sweet;
Grateful coolness in the heat;
Solace in the midst of woe.

O most blessed Light divine,
Shine within these hearts of yours,
And our inmost being fill!

Heal our wounds, our strength renew;
On our dryness pour your dew;
Wash the stains of guilt away:

Bend the stubborn heart and will;
Melt the frozen, warm the chill;
Guide the steps that go astray.

On the faithful, who adore
And confess you, evermore
In your sevenfold gift descend:

Give them virtue's sure reward;
Give them your salvation, Lord;
Give them joys that never end.

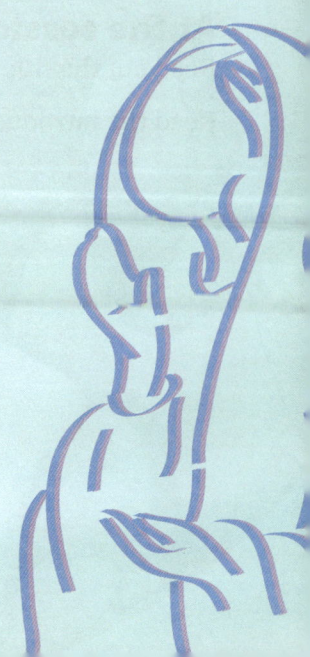

Leading Session 3: Why the Church?

Preparation

Read through session 3 carefully yourself, together with these notes, before the session, checking particularly that you understand the activities. Think about which sections you will ask participants to read. Practise the pronunciation of Latin-based words if you are not sure.

Photocopy a sufficient number of the 2 handouts for this session so that there is one for each person participating.

Bring to the session pens, pencils, some paper,

- a copy of the Bible, or preferably several, to be used for the scripture exercise.
- a copy of both volumes of the Documents of Vatican II
  volume 1 is useful for people who want to see the 16 conciliar documents
  volume 2 is useful for people who want to see the three post-conciliar documents on catechesis that are in it.
- a copy of the General Directory for Catechesis.
- a Catechism of the Catholic Church.

At this session a selection of encyclicals is highly recommended for the final activity. A handout is provided as a last resort, which is an example of what to look for in one document. It can be used if it is not possible to provide a variety of encyclicals for people to look at for themselves.

The following are the easiest documents for the activity for which they are required. It is useful to provide enough for people to work in groups of twos or threes.

- *Reconciliatio et paenitentia*
- *Dominum et vivificantem*
- *Christifideles laici*
- *Veritatis splendor*
- General Directory for Catechesis (not an encyclical but has many of the same features)

Prepare the room to provide a prayerful and welcoming atmosphere. Get refreshments ready.

At the session

Read out the title and Scripture quotation then say the prayer together.

Read the introductory paragraph or summarise it in your own words.

Echoes — Echoing Christ

Stop at the Numbered dots

1 Give out Handout 1 for everyone to work from, preferably in groups of twos or threes, though each with their own handout.

After about 5-10 minutes, help them to skim the text and quickly pick out the required information. They could mark the relevant places on the text.

This is not meant to be a laborious task. They can spend more time on it at home.

The table below gives you a summary of these stages found in Acts and sets out key points of how this process still happens today in the Church. You can highlight some of these if time allows or photocopy as a handout for their own use.

VERSES IN ACTS	COUNCIL OF JERUSALEM	SAME PROCESS TODAY
v.1-2	A problem arose and there were long arguments	This continues to happen
v.2	It was decided that Paul and Barnabas should go to Jerusalem to the apostles and elders	The problem is taken to a gathering of the successors of the apostles, bishops
v.3	All the members of the church were interested (saw them off)	Many of us are interested e.g. via the catholic newspapers for example
v.5	Converts want to continue their previous practice	This can happen today
v.6	They met and held a long discussion	Synods, councils and other meetings are held
v.7	Peter stood up and gave Christ's teaching	The successor of Peter speaks
v.12	Paul and Barnabas spoke about the evidence of peoples' lives changing	Other bishops and witnesses, (often lay experts in the subject) speak
v.13-15	James stood up and gave Scriptural roots to the decision	Scriptural roots underpin decisions
v.20	Let us send them a letter	Encyclicals and other types of teaching documents are published for the whole Church
v.22 & 27	And send delegates, men we highly respect	The Bishops are delegates for each diocese
v.22	The whole church agreed	The whole assembly agrees to the process and decision
v.25	The problem came from those acting without authority from us	Authority is with the bishops deciding together including the Pope
v.25	They decided unanimously. Elsewhere translated as 'came to one accord'	It is always important for an overwhelming majority of bishops to agree
v.28	To confirm by word of mouth what is written in the letter	When a new bishop or priest preaches, or talks are held, about a new encyclical letter or other document from Rome
	The decision was 'decided by the Holy Spirit and by ourselves'	Promise of the Holy Spirit's guidance into all the truth (John 16:13) taken seriously
v.31	When the letter was delivered the people were delighted with the encouragement it gave them	People are delighted with new encyclicals or clarification of teaching
v.35	Teaching of the Good News resumed	The teaching from Rome is followed in order to remain in truth and in unity

2 At this point, show the people a copy of volume 1 of the Documents of Vatican II.

You could explain that the Second Vatican Council took place in Rome during three autumnal sessions between 1962 and 1965. The outcome was a set of 16 agreed documents, the result of long discussions by the bishops in union with the Pope. Blessed Pope John Paul II called the Council 'this great gift of the Spirit to the Church'.

3 Give out handout 2 and explain that it is a diagram of all 16 documents of the Council with the four constitutions at the centre. It shows how they all relate to each other.

Go first to the centre of the diagram and you will see that there are two documents that are foundational to the Church at the very centre – one on the Liturgy and one on Revelation - and then, around these, two documents on the Church herself. These four are all called constitutions because they form the heart of the Council's teaching on the mystery of the Church.

You will then see three groups of four documents, these are either declarations or decrees, rather than constitutions (Check the Vatican council documents to find them and to see which are which) and they expand the teaching of the central four.

4 At this point it would be preferable for people to be able to look up the four constitutions for themselves in pairs in the Vatican documents. However at the bottom of handout 2 you will find the Latin titles and the first few lines of the text (in English) from where the title is drawn. Note that generally only the **first** word of the title starts with a capital letter, although there are a few exceptions.

- ***Sacrosanctum concilium*** – is the Latin for, 'sacred Council...'
- ***Lumen gentium*** – is the Latin for 'light' and 'humanity', 'Christ is the Light of humanity...'
- ***Dei Verbum*** – is the Latin for 'God's word', in the sentence, 'Hearing the Word of God...'
- ***Gaudium et spes*** – means 'The joy and hope...'

5 At this point you could show people the five documents, including Volume 2 of the Vatican II Documents for *Catechesi tradendae*, *Evangelii nuntiandi* and the first *General Catechetical Directory*. You will also have the other two present.

6 At this point, give out copies of different documents from Blessed Pope John Paul II for people to look at in order to answer some of the questions of the activity (all of the questions may be too many). The rest can be done at home if anyone has their own. If encyclicals cannot be acquired use handout 3 to follow the activity and in this case set all the questions.

After 5-10 minutes compare peoples' answers.

Conclude by reading out the summary and then say together the concluding prayer.

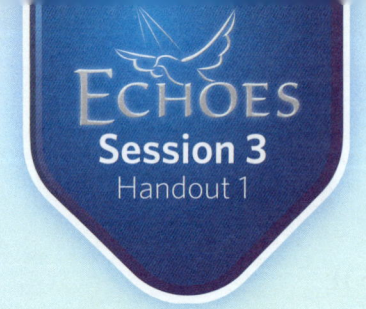

Controversy
Acts 15:1-35

1. Then some men came down for Judaea and taught the brothers, 'Unless you have yourselves circumcised in the tradition of Moses you cannot be saved'.
2. This led to disagreement, and after Paul and Barnabas had had a long argument with these men it was arranged that Paul and Barnabas and others of the church should go up to Jerusalem and discuss the problem with the apostles and elders.
3. All the members of the church saw them off and as they passed through Phoenicia and Samaria they told how the pagans had been converted, and this news was received with the greatest satisfaction
4. by the brothers. When they arrived in Jerusalem they were welcomed by the church and by the apostles and elders, and gave an account of all that God had done with them.
5. But certain members of the Pharisees' party who had become believers objected insisting that the pagans should be circumcised and instructed to keep the Law of Moses. The apostles and elders met to
6,7. look into the matter, and after the discussion had gone on a long time, Peter stood up and addressed them.

Speeches

'My brothers,' he said 'you know perfectly well that in the early days God made his choice among you: the pagans were to learn the Good News from me and so become believers. In fact God, who
8. can read everyone's heart, showed his approval of them by giving the Holy Spirit to them just as
9. he had to us. God made no distinction between them and us, since he purified their hearts by faith.
10. It would only provoke God's anger now, surely, if you imposed on the disciples the very burden that
11. neither we nor our ancestors were strong enough to support? Remember, we believe that we are saved in the same way as they are: through the grace of the Lord Jesus.'
12. This silenced the entire assembly, and they listened to Barnabas and Paul describing all the signs and wonders God had worked through them among the pagans.
13. When they had finished it was James who spoke. 'My brothers,' he said 'listen to me. Simeon has
14. described how God first arranged to enlist a people for his name out of the pagans. This is entirely
15. in harmony with the words of the prophets, since the scriptures say:
16. *After that I shall return and rebuild the fallen House of David;*
I shall rebuild it from its ruins and restore it.
17. *Then the rest of mankind, all the pagans who are consecrated to my name, will look for the Lord,*
18. *says the Lord who made this known so long ago.*
19. 'I rule, then, that instead of making things more difficult for pagans who turn to God, we
20. send them a letter telling them merely to abstain from anything polluted by idols, from
21. fornication, from the meat of strangled animals and from blood. For Moses has always had his preachers in every town, and is read aloud in the synagogues every Sabbath.'

The apostolic letter and delegates

22. Then the apostles and elders decided to choose delegates to send to Antioch with Paul and Barnabas; the whole church concurred with this. They chose Judas known as Barsabbas and Silas, both leading
23. men in the brotherhood, and gave them this letter to take with them:
'The apostles and elders, your brothers, send greetings to the brothers of pagan birth in Antioch,
24. Syria and Cilicia. We hear that some of our members have disturbed you with their demands and
25. have unsettled your minds. They acted without any authority from us, and so we have decided
26. unanimously to elect delegates and to send them to you with Barnabas and Paul, men we highly
27. respect who have dedicated their lives to the name of our Lord Jesus Christ. Accordingly we are
28. sending you Judas and Silas, who will confirm by word of mouth what we have written in this letter. It has been decided by the Holy Spirit and by ourselves not to saddle you with any burden beyond
29. these essentials; you are to abstain from food sacrificed to idols, from blood, from the meat of strangled animals and from fornication. Avoid these, and you will do what is right. Farewell.'
30. The party left and went down to Antioch, where they summoned the whole community and
31. delivered the letter. The community read it and were delighted with the encouragement it gave them.
32. Judas and Silas, being themselves prophets, spoke for a long time, encouraging and strengthening the
33. brothers. These two spent some time there, and then the brothers wished them peace and they went
35. back to those who had sent them. Paul and Barnabas, however, stayed on in Antioch, and there with many others they taught and proclaimed the Good News, the word of the Lord.

The Documents of Vatican II

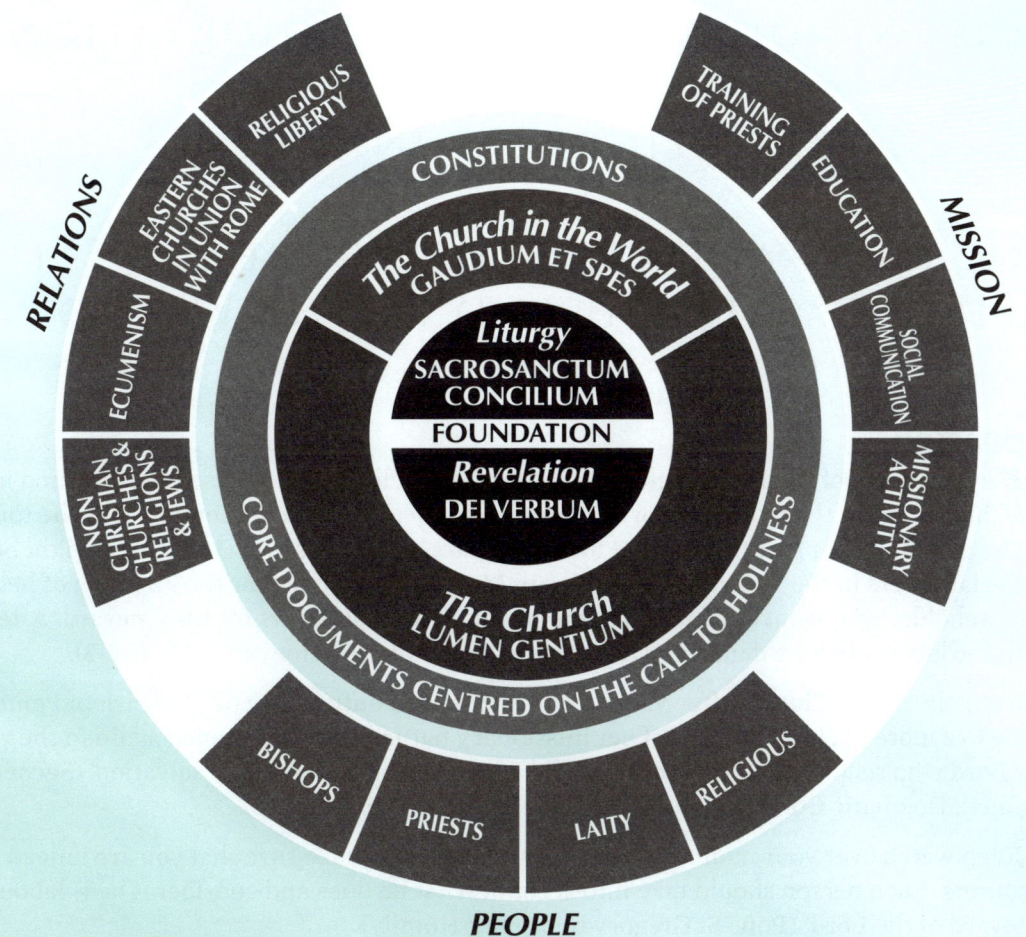

Diagram: Circular chart of Vatican II documents

- Centre (Foundation): Liturgy – SACROSANCTUM CONCILIUM; Revelation – DEI VERBUM
- Constitutions: The Church in the World – GAUDIUM ET SPES; The Church – LUMEN GENTIUM
- Core documents centred on the call to holiness
- RELATIONS: Religious Liberty; Eastern Churches in Union with Rome; Ecumenism; Non Christian Churches & Religions & Jews
- MISSION: Training of Priests; Education; Social Communication; Missionary Activity
- PEOPLE: Bishops; Priests; Laity; Religious

Latin titles and introductions of the Constitutions

- **SACROSANCTUM CONCILIUM** (4 December 1963)
  'The sacred Council has set out to impart an ever-increasing vigour to the Christian life of the faithful...'

- **LUMEN GENTIUM** (21 November 1964)
  'Christ is the Light of humanity...'

- **DEI VERBUM** (18 November 1965)
  'Hearing the Word of God with reverence, and proclaiming it with faith...'

- **GAUDIUM ET SPES** (7 December 1965)
  'The joy and hope, the anguish and grief of the men of our time, especially of those who are poor or afflicted in any way, are the joy and hope, the grief and anguish of the followers of Christ as well.'

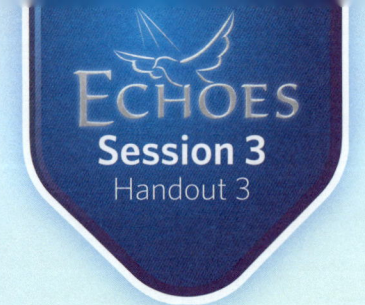

Christifideles Laici

Post-Synodal Apostolic Exhortation of His Holiness John Paul II on The Vocation and Mission of the Lay Faithful In the Church and in the World

Introduction

1. The lay members of Christ's faithful people (Christifideles Laici), whose 'Vocation and mission in the Church and in the world Twenty Years after the second Vatican Council' was the topic of the 1987 Synod of Bishops, are those who form that part of the people of God which might be likened to the labourers in the vineyard mentioned in Matthew's gospel: 'For the kingdom of heaven is like a householder who went out early in the morning to hire labourers for his vineyard. After agreeing with the labourers for a denarius a day, he sent them into his vineyard' (Mt 20:1-2).

2. ...In our times, the Church after Vatican II in a renewed outpouring of the Spirit of Pentecost has come to a more lively awareness of her missionary nature and has listened again to the voice of her Lord who sends her forth into the world as 'universal sacrament of salvation' (Second Vatican Council, Dogmatic Constitution on the Church, *Lumen gentium*, 48).

   ... 'Keep watch over your manner of life, dear people, and make sure that you are indeed the Lord's labourers. Each person should take into account what he does and consider if he is labouring in the vineyard of the Lord' (Pope St Gregory the Great, Homily).

At the end of the document, paragraph 64:

64. '...along with the Synod Fathers, the lay faithful present at the Synod and all other members of the people of God, I have recourse at the end of this post-synodal document to the Virgin Mary. At this moment this appeal becomes a prayer:

    O Most Blessed Virgin Mary,
    Mother of Christ and Mother of the Church,
    With joy and wonder we seek to make our own your Magnificat, joining you in your hymn of thankfulness and love...

Given at Rome, in St Peter's, on 30th December, the Feast of the Holy Family of Jesus, Mary and Joseph, in the year 1988, the eleventh of my pontificate.

Session 3

Why the Church?

'He who hears you, hears me'
(Lk 10:16)

Lord God, renew your Church with the Spirit of Wisdom and Love which you gave so fully to all the great teachers of your Church. Lead us by that same Spirit to seek you, the only fountain of true wisdom and the source of everlasting love. We ask this in the name of Jesus your Son, who lives and reigns with you and the Holy Spirit, world without end. Amen

In our last session we considered the way in which Christ is handed down to us in Scripture and Tradition.

In this session our focus is upon the Church as our mother and teacher. The teaching authority of the Church, the Magisterium, interprets Scripture and Tradition for us and speaks to us in the name of Christ. In this session we take time to explore this in more detail from the Second Vatican Council and the letters and writings of the Popes and Congregations in Rome.

The great grace of the Council

What a treasure there is, dear brothers and sisters, in the guidelines offered to us by the Second Vatican Council! ...With the passing of the years, the Council documents have lost nothing of their value or brilliance. They need to be read correctly, to be widely known and taken to heart as important and normative texts of the Magisterium, within the Church's Tradition. Now that the Jubilee has ended, I feel more than ever in duty bound to point to the Council as the great grace bestowed on the Church in the twentieth century: there we find a sure compass by which to take our bearings in the century now beginning.'

(Blessed Pope John Paul II, Novo millennio ineunte, At the Beginning of the New Millennium, 57)

Church Councils

What is the Second Vatican Council? In order to answer this question we need to understand what a Council is; and for this we need to go right back to the beginnings of the Church. We find the first Church Council recorded in the Acts of the Apostles as the beginnings of a system of decision-making. Major doctrinal, liturgical or moral problems were brought to a gathering of the Apostles and elders of the Christian communities. The problem was discussed, the situation was clarified, the truth was agreed and a decision was made. This was then communicated by letter to the Christian communities.

You can see this process described in Acts 15. In this chapter we have recorded for us the first of what have since been called ecumenical Councils. In two thousand years there have only been twenty-one such Councils, each named after the town in which it was held. The first is usually referred to as the Council of Jerusalem.

① **Read the story of the first Council in Acts 15:1-35. You will see distinct stages in the way this Council proceeds, and it is worth noting**

- **How and where the Apostles and elders met together (vv 2, 6)**
- **What the problem is which needs to be resolved (vv 1,5 & 25)**
- **The discussion of the problem and resolution of the problem (vv 6-22)**
- **How the decision is communicated to the Christian communities (vv 22-32)**

From the earliest times Church Councils have been held in order to resolve difficulties and to clarify the teaching of the Church on important matters. The records of their decisions have been handed down to us.

The Second Vatican Council

Now that we have looked at the role of Councils in the Church, let us consider the Second Vatican Council. This was the second Council to have been held at the Vatican, and it is therefore called the Second Vatican Council. Since this Council took place relatively recently – 1962-1965 – it is important that we learn more of what the Spirit has

② been saying to the Church of our time.

At this Council as many bishops as possible from the whole Church came together to confirm and clarify the faith that has come down to us from the Apostles. Never before have so many bishops from so many different continents and countries been able to gather together. So there never has been such a universal, ecumenical Council before.

Four key documents were drawn up by the Council. They are called 'Constitutions' to distinguish them from the many other documents that were produced. Like political constitutions, these set out fundamental principles about the life of Christ in the Church. The four are:

- The Constitution on the Sacred Liturgy (*Sacrosanctum concilium*)
- The Dogmatic Constitution on the Church (*Lumen gentium*)
- The Constitution on Divine Revelation (*Dei Verbum*)
- The Pastoral Constitution on the Church in the Modern World (*Gaudium et spes*)

③ Each of these documents has already been the occasion of a significant interior renewal in the Church. But the most profound renewal of the inner life of the Church can only be the result of a deep and spiritual taking to heart of the content of these documents.

Do not be alarmed at the Latin titles. It is the tradition of the Church to keep the official texts in Latin, not just for historical reasons but because Latin allows for exceptional clarity and precision. The first few words of the documents are taken as the title, and are normally deliberately chosen to indicate the key message or content of the text.

④ Look up the four 'Constitutions' mentioned above, and see this for yourself.

Then look back at what Blessed Pope John Paul said on the first page of the study sheet about the need to read the documents of Vatican II.

The most significant Council for us to come to know and love is the Second Vatican Council. Here the Spirit is speaking to us in our age through the Church.

Letters

The stages of the Council of Jerusalem that we noted above remain key elements in the Church's decision-making process. The Church today continues to teach us so that we can receive the Faith in a manner similar to that which we discovered when we read Acts chapter 15.

We have already seen that, following the Council of Jerusalem, other great Councils have been held throughout the history of the Church. Other features which we identified in the case of the Council of Jerusalem and which have remained constant are:

- **Letters**. Decisions of the Apostles continue to be communicated by letter. These letters are often called 'Apostolic Exhortation', 'Apostolic Letter' or simply 'Encyclical' (the Latin word for a circular 'letter').
- **The Scriptures.** At the Council of Jerusalem the Apostles were trying to discern what God had been saying to them through the Scriptures and in the life of the People of God. When you read Church documents and letters, you will notice how they also constantly refer to the Scriptures. When she teaches us, the Church draws her inspiration from this living source. Blessed Pope John Paul II, for example, usually begins his letters with a reflection upon a passage of Scripture. For example, the Apostolic Letter, *Novo millennio ineunte,* which we quoted at the beginning of this session, starts with a reference to the 'miraculous catch of fish' (Lk 5:4-6) and the Letter then weaves this theme throughout.

- **Tradition.** There is a tremendous reverence for Tradition in all of the Church's teaching. Church documents refer to previous knowledge in which the leaders of the Church have already come to one accord 'decided unanimously' (Acts 15:25). In most other subject areas, the knowledge of a hundred years ago has been superseded by later discoveries. Knowledge of the Faith is not like this. The Holy Spirit leads the Church into a deeper and broader understanding of God's Revelation given in Christ, but later centuries do not add anything onto the original Deposit of Faith as though the original Revelation was somehow incomplete. Hence, there is a respect, even reverence, shown at the beginning of many documents towards previous Church documents and gatherings because of the recognition that in them we find the unfolding of Tradition and the promised guidance of the Holy Spirit. In the Church, then, no document stands alone or contains an idea completely 'out of the blue'. It will always be in union with the body of truth built upon the teaching of the Apostles and deepened over the centuries. Again, we are aware of echoes, echoing Christ through time by the power of the Holy Spirit. It can be awe-inspiring to see the range of references being made in a document, spanning continents and centuries, and demonstrating the unity of the Catholic faith. In the last session you looked at the Catechism of the Catholic Church which is an extraordinary example of this.

5. **Following the same process there have been many issues raised about catechesis. These have been discussed at length in Rome and agreement reached and five very important post-conciliar documents (that is, since the Second Vatican Council) have been written:**

- The General Catechetical Directory (1971)
- *Evangelii nuntiandi* (Evangelisation in the Modern World) (1975)
- *Catechesi tradendae* (Catechesis in our Time) (1982)
- The Catechism of the Catholic Church (1992)
- The General Directory for Catechesis (1997)

We receive Christ and his Good News through letters written by the successors to the Apostles. These letters manifest a striking reverence for Scripture and Tradition, the sources of God's revelation.

Our Lady

We have focussed to some extent on the beginnings of Church documents. But we also have much to learn from the conclusions to Blessed Pope John Paul II's letters. At the end of each we find references to Our Lady.

The Second Vatican Council decided to include teaching about Our Lady in the Dogmatic Constitution on the Church, in the final chapter, which was called 'The Blessed Virgin Mary, Mother of God, in the mystery of Christ and the Church'. This reminds us that teaching about the Church is incomplete if it does not include Our Lady in her rightful place. The title of that chapter tells us that what the Catholic Faith believes about Mary is based on what it believes about Christ and about the Church, and what it teaches about Mary illumines in turn faith in both Christ and the Church. The way Blessed Pope John Paul II concludes all his teaching with reference to *her* reminds us of the balance we also need to keep in our teaching.

Why is there this close connection between Our Lady, Christ and the Church, so close that we cannot separate them? It is because Mary conceived by the Holy Spirit in her life, and Scripture tells us that she 'pondered' the mystery of Christ in her heart (Lk 2:19). In this keeping of the mystery of Christ in her heart she represents the Church which ponders the mystery over the centuries in order to bring Christ into the lives of each new generation. Thus Mary understands how very much we need the Spirit's divine enlightenment and transforming power as we participate in the Church's teaching ministry, united to the Apostles and their successors.

As catechists we commit ourselves into Mary's care. She is the Mother of Christ and the Church and our mother, too.

To conclude

Now, finally, look at one, or a range, of letters from the pen of Blessed Pope John Paul II and use these to identify a number of the features we have been considering.

(6) In this letter or range of letters from Blessed Pope John Paul II, note:

- **The kind of document that it is**
- **The Latin title and its meaning**
- **What the document is about**
- **The use of Scripture and the choice of the passages of Scripture**
- **The reverence for Tradition shown in introductory paragraphs and in footnotes**
- **The concluding reference to Our Lady**

Summary

In this third session we have been looking at:

- **The Second Vatican Council.**
- **Some characteristics of Church teaching documents.**
- **The Church as our teacher and our Mother and Our Lady's role in helping us to see this.**
- **Reasons why it is important to be familiar with Church documents.**

Further reading

- For the ways in which Christ is passed down to us in Scripture and Tradition: CCC 688.
- On the role of the Magisterium: CCC 888-892.
- On Our Lady and her significance: CCC 963-970.

Glossary on Councils and documents

Council: *a gathering of the bishops of the Church. The bishops are the successors of the Apostles and have been entrusted with guarding the deposit of faith, the teaching passed down by Christ to the Apostles. In Church Councils the bishops clarify and agree the meaning of aspects of the deposit of faith.*

Ecumenical Council: *When a Church Council is described as 'ecumenical' it is drawing on a Greek word meaning 'the whole inhabited world'*

Encyclical: *this simply means 'a circular letter'. An encyclical is a letter from the Pope to the Church, containing official teaching.*

Constitution, Dogmatic Constitution, Pastoral Constitution: *the four most important documents from the Second Vatican Council were called Constitutions, from the Latin* 'constituere', *'to establish.' These teachings, of a pastoral or doctrinal nature are highly significant, 'establishing' the Church in this area.*

Final Prayer

*Mary, Mother of the Redeemer,
as we venture further into the Third Millennium,
we ask that you will be for us the Star which
safely guides our steps to the Lord.
We ask this in the name of Jesus, your
Son and Lord. Amen.*

Leading Session 4: Why the Catechism?

Preparation
- Read carefully through session 4 together with these notes yourself before the session, checking particularly that you understand the activities. Think about which sections you will ask participants to read. Practise the pronunciation of Latin-based words if you are not sure.
- Photocopy a sufficient number of the 2 handouts for this session so that there is one for each person participating. Those who have a copy of the Catechism will not need the second handout.
- Bring to the session pens, pencils, some paper, and a copy of a Bible. Try to have several copies of the Catechism available to enable the participants to delve into the pages of the Catechism.
- Prepare the room to provide a prayerful and welcoming atmosphere. Get refreshments ready.

This session is to help catechists overcome any fears about the sheer size of the Catechism and give them practical guidance on how to use it for their own learning and for handing on the faith.

At the session
Read the title, followed by the sentence from Scripture, then *pray*.

Then read the introductory paragraph or summarise it in your own words.

Stop at the numbered dots

❶ Show participants the subject index. Explain that the numbers given there refer to the paragraphs in the Catechism, not the page numbers.

❷ Look at the logo together and ask the participants to identify the various symbols on the design and see whether they can interpret the meaning of these. Then turn to the explanation of the logo which is given inside the front cover of the Catechism.

❸ Using your own copy of the Catechism – and with others following if they can see a copy – leaf through the contents pages, stopping at each of the 4 parts to highlight the titles. Read together the second numbered point in this activity, which concerns the ordering of the 4 parts. Finally, go to the contents pages once more, drawing attention to the two sections in each part.

❹ Once you have completed the activity, move immediately to consider 'What's on a page', before reading 'Layout and Themes'. Go through the arrows, commenting briefly on each one:

'This tells you which of the four parts of the Catechism you are in'.
Which part of the Catechism is this page from? (The first part) What does the first part cover? (Faith and revelation and the Creed). This is from a section teaching about God as Almighty.

'Italicised words identify key teaching points, as do the bold sub-headings in the text.'
Can you find another italicized word? ('Mysterious'). The sub-headings identify the teaching points, which are then summarized by the italicised words. Thus, God's almighty power is a merciful, fatherly power; and it is a mysterious, apparently weak, power.

'When you are given a reference number….'
The Catechism has over two thousand paragraphs. The work is helpfully divided like this, with each paragraph containing one overall thought or idea.

'The central truths of the faith…'
You can mention that you are going to be reading about this point after you have finished looking at this page. You might want to check that everyone understands the meaning of the terms here, and look up 'Paschal Mystery' in the glossary if necessary.

'The Catechism emphasizes the implications for our lives…'
Explain here that the Catechism ends many of the sections with quotations from the saints in order to stress that these are the best guides we have for understanding and living the Faith.

'These numbers point us to the sources…'
Remember what Blessed Pope John Paul II said about catechesis renewed at the living sources of the faith. It is suggested that the sources are used for *study* (the catechist's own formation; to deepen awareness of what the text is saying; for *memorisation* (asking those we teach to memorise short sayings and verses from the Scriptures giving us spiritual wisdom we can draw upon easily, and *prayer* (use the Scriptural references, in particular, in one's prayer time and for *lectio divina*).

'Look for these words…'
The important point to reinforce here is that the Catholic Faith draws upon reason as well as revelation. We are not being asked blindly to accept the Faith; we are being invited to understand it as well.

'The numbers in italics at the side of the paragraphs…'
When planning teaching it is important to look up the side-references. These often take us to other parts of the Catechism, and you can remind participants that it is the four parts together which make up the Christian life. Following the cross-references into the four parts means that one is helping to see how life, worship and faith all link together.

❺ Once you have read the section on Layout and Themes up to this point, give out handout 1. This gives a pictorial representation of the structure and themes in the Catechism.

Structure
It is based on a Cross, to remind us that the work of Redemption is at the heart of the Catechism's presentation. The four parts of the Catechism are placed on the four points of the Cross. Under the heading of each part is given the subject matter of the second section of each part – Creed, Sacraments, Commandments, Our Father.

Themes
These have been placed in the middle, to show that they lie at the heart of each of the parts of the Catechism. The theme of The Church is placed slightly apart from the others because the faith itself is given to us by the Church.

At the foot of the page is the text of John 3:16, a classic text which is often thought to sum up the essence of the Gospel. This verse draws together all of the themes, and in so doing emphasizes for us that the Catechism, by having these themes at the heart of its presentation, has placed the basic Gospel message (the *kerygma*) at the very centre of its presentation of each aspect of the Faith.

❻ Give out handout 2. Give participants five minutes to read quietly to themselves. Then ask them to work, either on their own or in pairs, to identify the points given in the studysheet:

- which part they are in
- which paragraph numbers they are studying
- which sources are being used
- to which parts and aspects of the Catechism the side-references are linking us
- how the themes of Trinity, Christ, Redemption, dignity of the human person and Church are placed at the centre of the presentation.

Read the summary to consolidate the learning in the session and say together the *final prayer*.

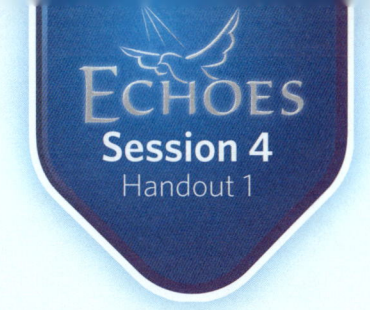

The Structure and Themes of the Catechism

Profession of Faith
Creed (Part 1)

THE CHURCH

- The Holy Trinity
- The Paschal Mystery
- Christ
- The Human Person

Celebration of Faith
Sacraments (Part 2)

Life in Christ
Commandments (Part 3)

Christian Prayer
Our Father (Part 4)

God so loved the world that he gave His only Son, so that everyone who has faith in him may not die but have eternal life (John 3:16)

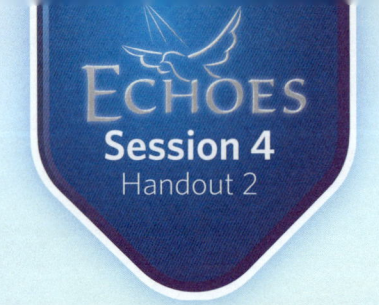

THE PROFESSION OF FAITH

III. God, 'He Who Is', Is Truth and Love

214 God, 'He Who Is', revealed himself to Israel as the one 'abounding in steadfast love and faithfulness'.[27] These two terms express summarily the riches of the divine name. In all his works God displays not only his kindness, goodness, grace and steadfast love, but also his trustworthiness, constancy, faithfulness and truth. 'I give thanks to your name for your steadfast love and your faithfulness.'[28] He is the Truth, for 'God is light and in him there is no darkness'; 'God is love', as the apostle John teaches.[29]

God is Truth

215 'The sum of your word is truth; and every one of your righteous ordinances endures forever.'[30] 'And now, O Lord God, you are God, and your words are true';[31] this is why God's promises always come true.[32] God is Truth itself, whose words cannot deceive. This is why one can abandon oneself in full trust to the truth and faithfulness of his word in all things. The beginning of sin and man's fall was due to a lie of the tempter who induced doubt of God's word, kindness and faithfulness.

216 God's truth is his wisdom, which commands the whole created order and governs the world.[33] God, who alone made heaven and earth, can alone impart true knowledge of every created thing in relation to himself.[34]

217 God is also truthful when he reveals himself – the teaching that comes from God is 'true instruction'.[35] When he sends his Son into the world it will be 'to bear witness to the truth':[36] 'We know that the Son of God has come and has given us understanding, to know him who is true.'[37]

God is Love

218 In the course of its history, Israel was able to discover that God had only one reason to reveal himself to them, a single motive for choosing them from among all peoples as his special possession: his sheer gratuitous love.[38] And thanks to the prophets Israel understood that it was again out of love that God never stopped saving them and pardoning their unfaithfulness and sins.[39]

219 God's love for Israel is compared to a father's love for his son. His love for his people is stronger than a mother's for her children. God loves his people more than a bridegroom his beloved; his love will be victorious over even the worst infidelities and will extend to his most precious gift: 'God so loved the world that he gave his only Son'.[40]

220 God's love is 'everlasting'.[41] 'For the mountains may depart and the hills be removed, but my steadfast love shall not depart from you.'[42] Through Jeremiah, God declares to his people, 'I have loved you with an everlasting love; therefore I have continued my faithfulness to you.'[43]

221 But St John goes even further when he affirms that 'God is love':[44] God's very being is love. By sending his only Son and the Spirit of Love in the fullness of time, God has revealed his innermost secret:[45] God himself is an eternal exchange of love, Father, Son and Holy Spirit, and he has destined us to share in that exchange.

---

[27] Ex 34:6
[28] Ps 138:2; cf Ps 85:11
[29] 1 Jn 1:5; 4:8
[30] Ps 119:160
[31] 2 Sam 7:28
[32] cf Dt 7:9
[33] cf Wis 13:1-9
[34] Cf Ps 115:15; Wis 7:17-21
[35] Mal 2:6
[36] Jn 18:37
[37] 1 Jn 5:20; cf Jn 17:3
[38] Cf Dt 4:37; 7:8; 10:15
[39] Cf Is 43:1-7; Hos 2
[40] Jn 3:16; Hos 11:1; Is 49:14-15; 62:4-5; Ezek 16; Hos 11;
[41] Is 54:8
[42] Is 54:10; cf 54:8
[43] Jer 31:3
[44] 1 Jn 4:8, 16
[45] cf 1 Cor 2:7-16; Eph 3:9-12

Session 4

Why the Catechism?

'Father... this is eternal life, that they may know You' (Jn 17:3)

Father, may the truth of the Gospel shine forth in your Church so that all are led by its beauty to seek you, the one God, and find everlasting life in your eternal Kingdom.
We ask this in the name of Jesus your Son, who lives and reigns with you and the Holy Spirit, world without end. Amen

In a previous session we discovered that a catechist is an echo of Christ and his Good News. We saw that the 'deposit of faith', as Scripture calls this treasure which is to be lovingly received and handed on, has been re-presented for our times in the Catechism of the Catholic Church. In this session we explore this Catechism. We look at its purpose, and how to use it for learning about the faith and for teaching the Faith.

The Catechism is a superbly-crafted teaching instrument. It is also a work that will transform your life and the lives of those you catechise. It is not a book to be read quickly; one needs to ponder the text, pray with it and immerse oneself in it to fully appreciate its visionary power and the compelling sense of beauty, goodness and truth which radiate from its pages. In these pages we meet the Spirit at work in his Church.

To read and use the Catechism prayerfully and carefully, searching its depths and allowing oneself to be questioned and challenged by its teaching, one needs to understand some of the elements which structure and inform its presentation of the faith. When these elements are firmly grasped and their significance appreciated the Catechism can become the most transforming and penetrating teaching tool the Church has ever possessed since the Scriptures.

Unfathomable riches

'I ask all the Church's Pastors and the Christian faithful to receive this Catechism in a spirit of communion and to use it assiduously in fulfilling their mission of proclaiming the faith and calling people to the Gospel life. This Catechism is given to them that it may be a sure and authentic reference text for teaching catholic doctrine... It is also offered to all the faithful who wish to deepen their knowledge of the unfathomable riches of salvation.'
Blessed Pope John Paul II, Fidei depositum, 'The Deposit of Faith'

The purpose of the Catechism

What do we learn about the Catechism from this excerpt from *Fidei depositum*?

① • **It is a sure reference guide.** It is reliable, a secure point to which we can turn to discover and understand Church teaching. You can use the contents pages or the indices to find out about particular aspects of Church teaching.

• **It proclaims faith.** It teaches the Faith clearly, unambiguously and fully. It is a serious presentation for adults of a living faith for today.

- **It calls us to the Gospel life, to Christ.** It is written to lead us to Christ and to life in him. The truths presented in its pages are truths about Christ. They lead us to communion with him.
- **It is a teaching tool.** The Catechism has been written to assist catechists, whether pastors or lay people. It is a teaching document. It is set out and structured for ease of teaching. It is the handbook every teacher of the Faith needs.

The logo on the front cover

2 Take a moment to look at the logo on the front cover of the Catechism. What is it? Look inside and read the explanation of the design. Notice how the logo presents the whole message of the Catholic Faith – Christ and His redemptive work are at the centre, redeemed humanity lies securely and peacefully at his feet, drawn into paradise to share the life of the Blessed Trinity. Christ is playing a beautiful melody, the 'symphony of the truth'.

This image of a **'symphony'** can help us to understand the **structure** and **layout** of the Catechism.

Structure

Just as a symphony normally has four movements, so the Catechism has four parts. These four parts correspond to the four 'parts', or dimensions, of the life of the Church and of every Christian. The Christian life is one of faith, worship, following Christ in the way we live, and prayer.

Catechism

3 1. **Turn to the Contents pages and *identify the four parts* of the Catechism.**

2. **Notice the *ordering of the four parts* and the *amount of space* given to each. Parts 1 and 2 proclaim God's Revelation and work, his loving Plan of Salvation, through the time of the Old Testament, the New Testament and now in the time of the Church when he works through the Liturgy and the Sacraments. This is what we have faith in and what we celebrate. Parts 3 and 4 are concerned with our response to God's gracious activity – our life in Christ and our prayer. God's action comes first (parts 1 and 2) and two-thirds of the Catechism is concerned with presenting this for us. Our action follows as a response to what God has done, and just one-third explains what we are to do. The Catechism, then, emphasises God's grace in the Christian life and asks catechists to do the same.**

3. **Notice that each part of the Catechism has *two sections*. The first section in each case looks at general issues and points concerned with faith, worship, morality and prayer. The second section focuses upon the Creed, the Sacraments, the Commandments and the Our Father.**

Layout and themes

A symphony is satisfying when it is experienced as a unified piece. A certain unity is achieved by the fact that the whole symphony is written in a particular musical key, C major, D minor, or whatever. Musical themes that are heard in one movement often recur in other movements.

We can think of the Catechism in a similar way. The authors of the Catechism tell us that 'This catechism is conceived as an *organic presentation* of the Catholic Faith in its entirety. It should therefore be seen as a unified whole.' (para 18) This is an important point. When we read a section of the Catechism we are doing more than learning about particular aspects of the Faith; the Catechism has been written so that, whichever page we open, we are introduced to the fullness of the Faith, to 'one thing' to be believed, to love and in which to place our hope. The Faith is one, though it is made up of many parts. This sense of unity is achieved in two ways in particular:

Through the use of cross-references. These link the different parts together to help us see connections between faith and life.

❹ What's on a page

> This tells you which of the four parts of the Catechism you are in.

> Italicised words identify key teaching points, as do the bold sub-headings in the text.

> When you are given a reference number for the Catechism, it is not the page number, but the paragraph number. All Church documents use this method of referencing. 'CCC' is the abbreviation used for the Catechism, so 'CCC 271' is paragraph number 271 in the Catechism.

> The central truths of the Faith stand at the heart of every part of the Catechism: Christ, the Paschal Mystery, the Holy Trinity, the Church and the dignity of every human person.

> The Catechism emphasises the implications for our lives of the Faith we profess, and provides models for us to contemplate.

> These numbers point us to the sources which are listed at the foot of the page. Notice how the majority are from the Scriptures. Catechists can use these references for study, for memorisation and for prayer.

> The numbers in italics at the side of the paragraphs are cross-references to other paragraphs. These shed more light on the topic you are considering. They expand points, link the parts together, and help to deepen our understanding of the topic we are investigating.

> Look for these words – 'therefore', 'because', 'thus', 'for', and so on – which indicate that reasons are being given for the statement which has just been made. The Catechism explains the Faith as well as presenting it.

Page content shown (CCC excerpt, p. 64, THE PROFESSION OF FAITH):

history, governing hearts and events in keeping with his will: 'It is always in your power to show great strength, and who can withstand the strength of your arm?'[107]

'You are merciful to all, for you can do all things'[108]

270 God is the *Father* Almighty, whose fatherhood and power shed light on one another: God reveals his fatherly omnipotence by the way he takes care of our needs; by the filial adoption that he gives us ('I will be a father to you, and you shall be my sons and daughters, says the Lord Almighty'):[109] finally by his infinite mercy, for he displays his power at its height by freely forgiving sins.

271 God's almighty power is in no way arbitrary: 'In God, power, essence, will, intellect, wisdom, and justice are all identical. Nothing therefore can be in God's power which could not be in his just will or his wise intellect.'[110]

The mystery of God's apparent powerlessness

272 Faith in God the Father Almighty can be put to the test by the experience of evil and suffering. God can sometimes seem to be absent and incapable of stopping evil. But in the most mysterious way God the Father has revealed his almighty power in the voluntary humiliation and Resurrection of his Son, by which he conquered evil. Christ crucified is thus 'the power of God and the wisdom of God. For the foolishness of God is wiser than men, and the weakness of God is stronger than men.'[111] It is in Christ's Resurrection and exaltation that the Father has shown forth 'the immeasurable greatness of his power in us who believe'.[112]

273 Only faith can embrace the mysterious ways of God's almighty power. This faith glories in its weaknesses in order to draw to itself Christ's power.[113] The Virgin Mary is the supreme model of this faith, for she believed that 'nothing will be impossible with God', and was able to magnify the Lord: 'For he who is mighty has done great things for me, and holy is his name.'[114]

274 'Nothing is more apt to confirm our faith and hope than holding it fixed in our minds that nothing is impossible with God. Once our reason has grasped the idea of God's almighty power, it

---

[107] *Wis* 11:21; cf. *Esth* 4:17b; *Prov* 21:1; *Tob* 13:2.
[108] *Wis* 11:23.
[109] *2 Cor* 6:18; cf. *Mt* 6:32.
[110] St Thomas Aquinas, *STh* I, 25, 5, ad 1.
[111] *1 Cor* 1:24-25.
[112] *Eph* 1:19-22.
[113] Cf. *2 Cor* 12:9; *Phil* 4:13.
[114] *Lk* 1:37, 49.

Side references: 2777; 1441; 309, 412, 609; 648; 148; 1814, 1817

Through the use of recurring 'themes' which lie at the heart of the Faith. We can call these the 'foundational truths' of the Faith. They run like golden threads through each part of the Catechism. They are:

- The Holy Trinity
- The Person of Christ, true God and true Man
- The Paschal Mystery, the saving death and Resurrection of Christ
- The nature and dignity of the human person, created and graced
- **(5)** The Church

One of the keys to effective teaching with the Catechism is to ensure that, whatever the subject you are teaching, you relate it to these key themes. Why? First, because in doing this you will be helping others to see the coherence of the faith, the way in which the pieces fit together. Secondly, because you will be offering your hearers reasons for the Faith: the Church's teaching becomes understandable in that the elements you are teaching are seen to be drawn together in a beautiful harmony around these themes.

(6) Read paragraphs 214-221: 'God, He Who Is, is Truth and Love'.

Look for the points raised in this session.

Summary

In this third session we have been looking at:

- **Why the Catechism is so important for catechists.**
- **How to use the Catechism to learn about the Faith.**
- **How to use the Catechism to teach the Faith.**

Further reading

- For the purpose of the Catechism: *'Fidei depositum'*, Blessed Pope John Paul II's introduction to the Catechism.
- For how to learn from the Catechism and teach the Faith from it: the Prologue, 1-25; and the General Directory for Catechesis, Part Two, Chapter Two.
- CCC 1996-1999: The Catechism on grace.

Glossary on some key terms in the new Catechism

Fidei depositum: 'Deposit of Faith', the title given by Blessed Pope John Paul II to his introduction to the Catechism

Grace: is a participation in the life of God, a free and undeserved gift. God's infinite love, always above and beyond us, but also revealed and therefore knowable by us to some extent

Mystery: the reality of God lying at the heart of creation and especially of the history of salvation which we know only because God has revealed himself to us

Paschal Mystery: the phrase used to describe the reality of our redemption through Christ's passion, Resurrection and Ascension, a redemption of which we know because God has revealed this to us.

Final meditation and prayer

O my God, Trinity whom I adore, help me to forget myself entirely so as to establish myself in you, unmovable and peaceful as if my soul were already in eternity. May nothing be able to trouble my peace or make me leave you, O my unchanging God, but may each minute bring me more deeply into your mystery!
Blessed Elizabeth of the Trinity (see CCC 260)

Glory be to the Father, and to the Son and to the Holy Spirit. As it was in the beginning, is now, and ever shall be, world without end. Amen.

Leading Session 5 – 'Who Teaches?'

Preparation
- **Read** through session 5 carefully yourself, together with these notes, before the session, checking particularly that you understand the activities. Think about which sections you will ask participants to read. Practise the pronunciation of Latin-based words if you are not sure.
- **Photocopy** a sufficient number of the handout for this session so that there is one for each person participating.
- **Bring** to the session: pens, pencils, some paper,
- a copy of the Bible, or preferably several, to be used for the Scripture exercise.
- a copy of the *General Directory for Catechesis.*
- a *Catechism of the Catholic Church.*
- Prepare the room to provide a prayerful and welcoming atmosphere.
- Get refreshments ready.

At the Session
Have the title and the scripture quotation read out then say together the *opening prayer*.
Explain briefly what the session is about from the introductory paragraph.

Stop at the numbered dots

❶ Using the handout provided, ask the group members to take turns in reading out the Scripture text from the Gospel of St. John to hear the words of union and dependence. Tell people to stop for a few minutes in silence. Remind them that there is plenty of space on the handout for them to mark the text and add their own notes.

❷ Make sure people are looking for *ways and means* of abiding and being transformed. These begin, of course, in Baptism but help them also to think more practically of ways for today, for adults and children. The catechist is called to hand on faith in Christ, not mere information, and that faith needs to be nourished and helped to hold firm. Suggestions will include: going to Mass, the Sacrament of Penance, and other sacraments; praying every day, going to other devotions such as the Rosary or Stations of the Cross or parish talks, helping others such as in parish groups and activities; reading spiritual books – **make suggestions**.

❸ As Jesus can only do his work in communion with the Father, enabling the Father to speak through him, so we can only do Christ's work by being in communion with Christ. Ask the group to listen carefully to these adaptations, perhaps closing their eyes, while you read them slowly, emphasising 'you'.

- Jesus says to us: 'Truly, truly, I say to you, you can do nothing on your own accord, but only what you see me doing, for whatever I do, you can do likewise.'
- You can do nothing on your own, you can judge justly only because you seek my will and not your own.
- He who eats me will live because of me.
- Do you not believe that I am in you and you are in me, and so, speak my words and let me work through you.
- The Father himself loves you, because you have loved me and have believed that I came from the Father. Amen.

Continue with the text of the studysheet, conclude with the summary and say together the concluding meditation and prayer.

Jesus and his Father

"In all truth I tell you,
  by himself the Son can do nothing;
  he can only do what he sees the Father doing:
  and whatever the Father does the Son does too."

John 5:19

"By myself I can do nothing;
  I can judge only as I am told to judge,
  and my judging is just,
  because I seek to do not my own will
  but the will of him who sent me."

John 5:30

"As the living Father sent me
  and I draw life from the Father,
  so whoever eats me will also draw life from me."

John 6:57

"What I say
  is what the Father has taught me;
  he who sent me is with me,
  and has not left me to myself,
  for I always do what pleases him."

John 8:29

"For I have not spoken of my own accord;
  but the Father who sent me
  commanded me what to say and what to speak,
  and I know that his commands mean eternal life.
  And therefore what the Father has told me
  is what I speak."

John 12:49-50

"Do you not believe
  that I am in the Father and the Father is in me?
  What I say to you I do not speak of my own accord:
  it is the Father, living in me, who is doing his works."

John 14:10

Session 5

Who Teaches?

As the Father sent me so I send you (John 20:21)

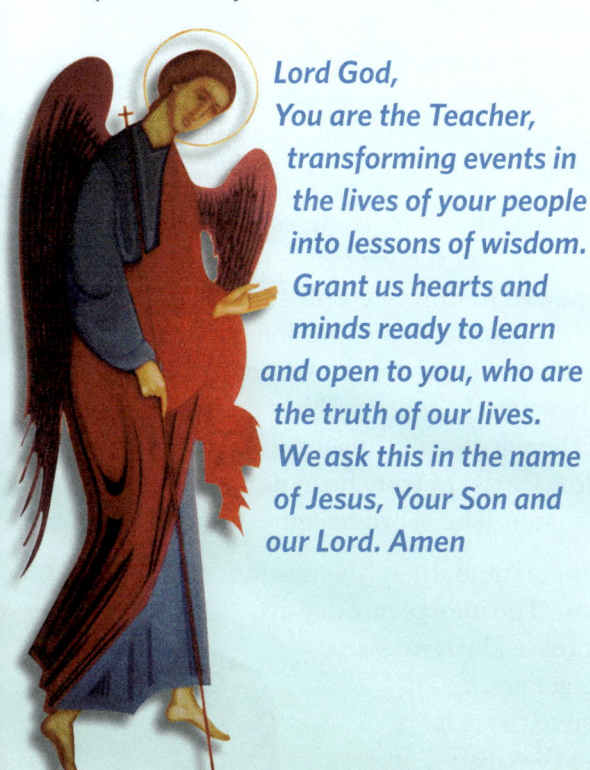

*Lord God,
You are the Teacher, transforming events in the lives of your people into lessons of wisdom. Grant us hearts and minds ready to learn and open to you, who are the truth of our lives. We ask this in the name of Jesus, Your Son and our Lord. Amen*

The purpose of this session is to focus on the supreme Catechist, God himself. We rightly think of God as the subject matter of our catechesis: our teaching is about him. What we can easily forget, though, is that the three Persons of the Blessed Trinity are also actively present in the mind and heart of the *catechist*, in the work of *catechesis* and in the lives of those being *catechised*. As catechists we are deeply privileged in being able to share in what is essentially a divine work. This session will make clear how much you can rely on God's presence and providence in all catechetical activities.

Let go and let God

'There is a temptation which perennially besets every spiritual journey and pastoral work: that of thinking that the results depend on our ability to act and to plan. God, of course, asks us really to co-operate with his grace...'
Blessed Pope John Paul II, NMI 38

God the Father: the Source of catechesis

God the Father is the Source of all that is. He is the Source of the divine life of the Trinity. The infinite life of the Trinity overflows, through sheer love and joy, into the act of creation. The Father, then, is the Source of everything that exists, and he wishes to give us, not only a share in creation, but a share in his very own life.

From the first moment of our creation, therefore, God has been working to draw us to himself. The principal way in which he has done this has been by **revealing** himself and his unchanging plan to draw us into his life of happiness.

God has revealed himself by sending his Son, who shares in his own substance and being. The source of our catechesis, then, lies in the Father's desire to share his life with us. And this is why all catechesis is rooted in Divine Revelation.

The Scriptures speak to us of God's desire that we should come to know him and his love for us:

'In many and various ways God spoke of old to our fathers by the prophets; but in these last days he has spoken to us by a Son, whom he appointed the heir of all things.' (Hebrews 1:1)

This text emphasises that **everything starts with God's imaginative initiative** ('In many and various ways') of entering into **dialogue** ('God spoke') for the sake of a **relationship** with his people ('to us').

God teaches us in stages. First he teaches through the prophets, and then he teaches fully through the Son, the Word made flesh. Through the prophets God says,

'Incline your ear, and come to me; hear that your soul may live' (Is.55:3).

And through the sending of his Son he calls out to us:

'This is my beloved Son, with whom I am well pleased: listen to him' (Matthew 17:5).

In catechesis, then, it is God who is constantly at work, making himself known.

Catechesis has its source in the Father's loving initiative to reveal himself and his plan by sending his Son.

Christ, sent by the Father

God **speaks** and **acts** in the person of Christ, who is the **Word** made **flesh**. In the person of Christ God has told us everything that he wants to say. Not only does Christ, like the prophets, speak words *from* God and *about* God, He *is* the Word of God. Not only does Christ, like the prophets before him and the saints after him, act as God wishes, He *is* God, acting in the flesh.

Christ is the bringer of the Good News, and he is the Good News itself. He teaches about God and his Kingdom, and he is himself the presence of God and his Kingdom among us. This is why he calls himself 'the Way and the Truth and the Life' (Jn 14:6).

1 **Look at the following Scripture references from the Gospel of St. John showing Christ's union with the Father and his utter dependence upon him.**
- **5:19, 30**
- **6:57**
- **8:29**
- **12:49-50**
- **14:10, 24**

Pick out key words which indicate Christ's *union* with the Father and his *dependence* on him.

We have seen that the Father wants to establish a relationship with each person. He does this through sending God the Son. This is why the Church speaks of **communion** with Christ as the purpose of catechesis, because it is in and through communion with Christ that we are in communion with the Blessed Trinity. The Catechism opens with this verse from St John's Gospel: 'this is eternal life, that they know you, the only true God, and Jesus Christ whom you have sent.' (17:3)

Christ is at the centre of our teaching. The Church describes catechesis as 'Christocentric', 'Christ-centred'. In *Catechesi tradendae* we read:

- 'At the heart of catechesis we find, in essence, a person, the person of Jesus of Nazareth' (CT 5).
- 'In catechesis it is Christ... who is taught... everything else is taught in reference to him... and it is Christ alone who teaches... anyone else teaches to the extent that he is Christ's spokesman, enabling Christ to teach with his lips' (CT 6).

Christ is whom we teach. In a profound sense, Christ is also the Teacher, in fact the only true Teacher (cf. Mt 23:10). Catechesis has a divine source, accessible only through Christ who has come 'from above', as St John puts it (3:31). And so, as catechists, we are only teachers in so far as we live **in Christ**. Jesus said, 'Abide in me, and I in you... for apart from me you can do nothing' (Jn 15:4,5).

If we abide in Christ and live in communion with him in his Church we can teach with minds renewed in him (see Eph 4:23). Our teaching then flows from a relationship with Christ and knowledge of him. We teach effectively when the love of Christ controls our lives and the wisdom of Christ rules our minds. As we allow Christ to transform us, our lives and teaching match. The Word becomes flesh in us.

We can understand, then, the wisdom of Paul VI's words, 'The men of our day are more impressed by witnesses than by teachers, and if they listen to these it is because they also bear witness' (*Evangelii nuntiandi* 41).

② **To discuss together:** What are the means by which we can abide in Christ and continue to be transformed by Christ?

③ **Listen** to the following adaptations from St John's Gospel. They will be read to you slowly and meditatively so that you can reflect on what it means to abide in Christ.

In catechesis it is Christ who is taught and Christ who teaches. The catechist abides in Christ.

The Holy Spirit

We have looked at the role of the Father as source of all revelation and Christ who was sent by the Father to reveal fully the mind, heart and plan of God. We have also seen that we are invited not simply to *learn from* him but also to *live in* him. In order to enable us to know Christ and to live in him, the Holy Spirit was sent to guide the Apostles.

In describing this mission that the Spirit would have in the Church, Christ used the significant words: 'The Holy Spirit whom the Father will send in my name will teach you everything and remind you of all I have said to you.' (Jn 14:26). And, he added: 'When the Spirit of Truth comes, he will lead you to the complete truth...' (Jn 16:13).

The Spirit is thus promised to the Church and to each Christian as an interior Teacher, who, through the light of faith, helps each person to grasp the reality of the truths of the Faith. The Holy Spirit is the Divine Teacher in every catechetical situation. Pope Paul VI therefore reminds us that we can never 'dispense with the secret action of the Holy Spirit' (EN 75).

Catechesi tradendae sums up these points when it says that, 'when carrying out her mission of giving catechesis, the Church – and also every individual Christian devoting himself to that mission within the Church and in her name – must be very much aware of acting as a living pliant instrument of the Holy Spirit. To invoke the Spirit constantly, to be in communion with Him... must be the attitude of the teaching Church and of every catechist' (CT 72).

The Holy Spirit is the interior Teacher of the Faith.

The Church

We have looked briefly at the role of the Persons of the Trinity in the work of catechesis. We must not forget the Church. The *General Directory for Catechesis* links the Church directly to the Holy Spirit in its heading: 'The transmission of Revelation by the Church, the work of the Holy Spirit' (GDC 42).

Catechesis is ecclesial (meaning 'of the Church') because the Holy Trinity continues its mission through the Church, of drawing humanity into the fullness of redemption. The *General Directory for Catechesis* says that, 'Continuing the mission of Christ and animated by the Holy Spirit, the Church is *the* teacher of the Faith. Catechesis is understood as an essentially ecclesial act' (GDC 78).

These are strong words and important for us to reflect upon. The Church transmits the Faith which she herself lives and, by this life and transmission, not only helps those being catechised, but also 'brings the community itself to maturity' (GDC 221).

Catechesis is also ecclesial because the Faith is always handed on in and through the Church. As individual Catholics, we have received the Faith of the Church and we now share in the passing on of this Faith.

Finally, catechesis is ecclesial because it is through the sacraments that we receive the grace we need to go out and spread the word. In this sacramental sense too, catechesis in the Faith of the Church is above all a work of grace and of the Church.

We join with the Holy Trinity and the Church in our work of catechesis.

Summary

In this fifth session we have been looking at:

- **The work of the Trinity in the catechist, in the work of catechesis, and in the lives of those being catechised.**
- **The desire and plan of the Father to draw us to himself through sending his Son among us.**
- **What it means to be 'in Christ', with Christ as the centre of catechesis.**
- **The work of the Holy Spirit in catechesis, in and through the Church.**

Further reading

On God the Father as the Source of catechesis:

- The opening paragraphs (1-4) of the Second Vatican Council document on Revelation, *Dei Verbum,* together with the Catechism 50-53, give us a clear presentation on why the Father wants to reveal himself to us and how he does this. The Scriptures emphasise the ways in which God continually intervenes to turn events into occasions of grace and wisdom. On this, read Jer 31:3 and Psalms 3, 18, 34, 81, 86, and 95.

On God the Son as the fullness of Truth:

- CCC 65, 428-9: give excellent summaries of this.
- GDC 40-41, 140: explain why catechesis must be Christocentric and examine the way in which Christ himself taught.
- CT 5-9: offers profound teaching on Christ the Catechist.

On God the Holy Spirit as the interior Teacher:

- CT 72 and GDC 142: examine the action of the Holy Spirit as the interior Teacher.
- CCC 683-686: explains the role of the Holy Spirit in awakening faith and ongoing conversion.

Glossary on the Trinity

Trinity: One God in three persons, Father, Son and Holy Spirit, the central mystery of the Christian Faith.

Revelation: to make accessible or visible what was hidden. God reveals himself, makes himself known.

Communion: literally, 'union with.' The Divine Persons live in eternal communion, in union with each other.

Christocentric: Christ-centred.

Christocentric catechesis: catechesis centred on Christ.

Ecclesial: relating to the Church. The Church is the work of the Blessed Trinity, who fills her with grace.

Abbreviations

From now on we will be using these abbreviations for the documents we have been considering:

CCC	Catechism of the Catholic Church
CT	Catechesi tradendae
DV	Dei Verbum
EN	Evangelii nuntiandi
GDC	General Directory for Catechesis

Final meditation and prayer

'Whoever is called to teach Christ must first seek "the surpassing worth of knowing Christ Jesus", he must suffer "the loss of all things..." in order to gain "Christ and be found in him..." ' (CCC 428)

God be in my head and in my understanding.
God be in my eyes and in my looking.
God be in my mouth and in my speaking.
God be in my heart and in my thinking.
God be at my end and
at my departing. Amen.

Leading Session 6: Whose Story?

Preparation

- **Read** through session 6 carefully yourself, together with these notes, before the session, checking particularly that you understand the activities. Think about which sections you will ask participants to read. Practise the pronunciation of Latin-based words if you are not sure.

- **Photocopy** a sufficient number of the handouts for this session so that there is one for each person participating. Those who have a copy of the Catechism will not need the final handout.

- **Bring** to the session: pens, pencils, some paper,

- a copy of the Bible, or preferably several, to be used for the Scripture exercise.

- a missal

- a *Catechism of the Catholic Church.*

- **Prepare the room** to provide a prayerful and welcoming atmosphere.

- Get refreshments ready.

This session is to help catechists to explore the Story of Salvation. The role of the catechist is to share with others this story of God's never-ending love. It is a story with which they will be familiar in outline, and this session will consolidate this for them and give them confidence to see the overall 'shape' of the faith, with a strong sense of the beginning and end of all things in God. We will also look at how the story impacts on our catechesis.

At the session

Read the title, followed by the sentence from Scripture, and then *pray*.
Then read the introductory paragraph or summarise it in your own words to introduce the session.

Stop at the numbered dots

❶ This is a wonderful story to read, focusing as it does on the transformation of the disciples in their encounter with the risen Christ. After you, or someone in the group, have read the passage, read through the blue comment on it. Highlight the sentence in the passage from Luke which tells us that Jesus explained the whole Story with reference to himself: 'Then starting with Moses and going through all the prophets....' The text makes it clear that it is the whole of the Scriptures that are interpreted by reference to himself. You may want to conclude this activity by asking participants whether they can see the links in this passage of Scripture to the Mass. They may be able to see the two parts of the Mass – the Liturgy of the Word and the Liturgy of the Eucharist (see CCC 1346-1347).

❷ After reading the heading, 'Telling the Story', give out Handout 1. This provides a simple, pictorial summary of the story, in even clearer outline than is given on the studysheet. You might like to explain the alpha and omega, the beginning and end, symbols on the handout – the Story begins and ends in God. Then comment that we are living in the third stage of the Story, in the era when we wait in hope. Remind participants of the phrase 'waiting in joyful hope' used at Mass.

You can now read the more detailed account on the studysheet. It is fairly self-explanatory, though at any of the points you may want to stop and add a comment. It is good to simply read it through once, however, so that people can get an overview. After this you can go back and look at any particular points.

You may want to comment on the fact that God is a 'family', and that the human race is also described as a fallen 'family' and a 'family' with a new identity after Pentecost. Redemption is about joining God's family as adopted sons and daughters.

❸ For the activity, 'Identifying the Parts', there are two well-known texts which will reinforce for us the outline of the story – the Creed and the Fourth Eucharistic Prayer. Use Handout sheets 2 and 3, use these to find the three stages of the Story.

In the case of **the Creed**, ask participants to see how it is Trinitarian in shape, and related to the phases of creation, redemption and sanctification. Point out the clear beginning, middle and end of the story.

In the case of the extract from the **Eucharistic Prayer**, it is important that the prayer, like the Creed (and like the summary of the Story on the studysheet) begins with God in himself. God is a family, a Trinity of Persons, *in himself*. He did not need to create. He is Father, Son and Spirit *in* and *for* himself. Through all eternity he lives in 'unapproachable light'. The section, 'Praise to the Father', contains the whole Story, from beginning to end, and it would be good to read this together.

❹ Give out handout 4 to those who do not have a Catechism with them. Focus on the three sub-headings – these give us the three stages of the Story. CCC 1218 begins with Creation, and the following paragraphs link the sacrament to parts of the Story in the Old Testament. Then 1223 connects Baptism to the centre of the Story, to the life of Christ. Finally, 1226 speaks of Baptism since Pentecost, the beginning of the third part of the story. We can see from this example how helpful it is to have the outline of the Story of Salvation within which we can place our understanding of doctrine.

After this exercise, the final part of the session is looking at various ideas about using the Story in catechesis. Depending upon the amount of time you have left, these can be points where you stop to discuss the possibilities presented and reflect upon the experience of those present concerning ways in which they have used the story in their teaching.

Read the *summary* and say together the *final prayer*.

The Story of Salvation

Alpha

THE FIRST STAGE

THE TIME OF THE PROMISES	→ CREATION → FALL → THE OLD COVENANT → THE PROMISES OF THE NEW COVENANT

THE SECOND STAGE

THE FULLNESS OF TIME	☧ INCARNATION LIFE PASSION DEATH RESURRECTION ASCENSION

THE THIRD STAGE

THE TIME OF THE CHURCH, WAITING IN HOPE	→ PENTECOST → THE HISTORY OF THE CHURCH, LIFE IN CHRIST AND IN THE SPIRIT → THE TIME OF EXPECTATION → THE SECOND COMING

Omega

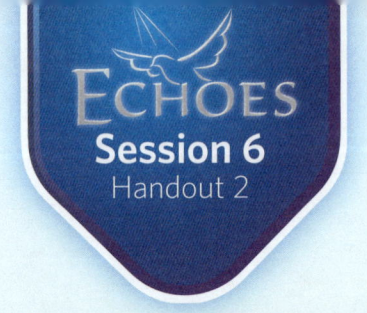

The Nicene Creed

I believe in one God,
    the Father almighty,
    maker of heaven and earth,
    of all things visible and invisible.

I believe in one Lord Jesus Christ,
    the Only Begotten Son of God,
    born of the Father before all ages.
    God from God, Light from Light,
    true God from true God,
    begotten, not made,
    consubstantial with the Father;
    through him all things were made.

    For us men and for our salvation
        he came down from heaven,
    and by the Holy Spirit
        was incarnate of the Virgin Mary,
        and became man.
    For our sake he was crucified under Pontius Pilate,
        he suffered death and was buried,
        and rose again on the third day
        in accordance with the Scriptures.
        He ascended into heaven
        and is seated at the right hand of the Father.
        He will come again in glory to judge the living and the dead
        and his kingdom will have no end.

I believe in the Holy Spirit, the Lord, the giver of life,
    who proceeds from the Father and the Son,
    who with the Father and the Son is adored and glorified,
    who has spoken through the prophets.
    I believe in one, holy, catholic and apostolic Church.
    I confess one Baptism for the forgiveness of sins
    and I look forward to the resurrection of the dead
    and the life of the world to come. Amen.

The opening of Eucharistic Prayer IV

Preface
It is truly right to give you thanks,
truly just to give you glory, Father most holy,
for you are the one God living and true,
existing before all ages and abiding for all eternity,
dwelling in unapproachable light;
yet you, who alone are good, the source of life,
have made all that is, so that you might fill your creatures with blessings
and bring joy to many of them by the glory of your light.
And so, in your presence are countless hosts of Angels, who serve you day and night and, gazing upon
the glory of your face, glorify you without ceasing.
With them we, too, confess your name in exultation,
giving voice to every creature under heaven as we acclaim:

Sanctus
Holy, Holy, Holy Lord God of hosts.
Heaven and earth are full of your glory.
Hosanna in the highest.
Blessed is he who comes in the name of the Lord.
Hosanna in the highest.

Praise to the Father
We give you praise, Father most holy, for you are great,
and you have fashioned all your works in wisdom and in love.
You formed man in your own image and entrusted the whole world to his care,
so that in serving you alone, the Creator, he might have dominion over all creatures.
And when through disobedience he had lost your friendship, you did not abandon him to the domain of death.
For you came in mercy to the aid of all, so that those who seek might find you.
Time and again you offered them covenants and through the prophets taught them to look forward to salvation.
And you so loved the world, Father most holy,
that in the fullness of time you sent your Only Begotten Son to be our Saviour.
Made incarnate by the Holy Spirit and born of the Virgin Mary,
he shared our human nature in all things but sin.
To the poor he proclaimed the good news of salvation, to prisoners, freedom,
and to the sorrowful of heart, joy.
To accomplish your plan, he gave himself up to death, and, rising from the dead, he destroyed
death and restored life.
And that we might live no longer for ourselves but for him who died and rose again for us,
he sent the Holy Spirit from you, Father, as the first fruits for those who believe,
so that, bringing to perfection his work in the world, he might sanctify creation to the full.

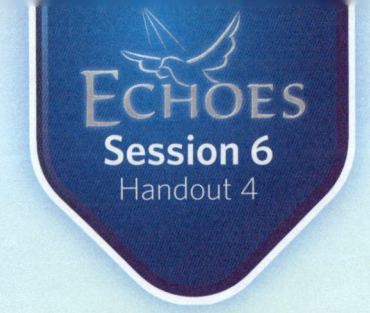

II. Baptism in the Economy of Salvation

Prefigurations of Baptism in the Old Covenant

1217 In the liturgy of the Easter Vigil, during the blessing of the baptismal water, the Church solemnly commemorates the great events in salvation history that already prefigured the mystery of Baptism:

> Father, you give us grace through sacramental signs,
> which tell us of the wonders of your unseen power.
>
> In Baptism we use your gift of water,
> which you have made a rich symbol
> of the grace you give us in this sacrament.

1218 Since the beginning of the world, water, so humble and wonderful a creature, has been the source of life and fruitfulness. Sacred Scripture sees it as 'overshadowed' by the Spirit of God.

> At the very dawn of creation
> your Spirit breathed on the waters,
> making them the wellspring of all holiness.

1219 The Church has seen in Noah's ark a prefiguring of salvation by Baptism, for by it 'a few, that is, eight persons, were saved through water':

> The waters of the great flood
> you made a sign of the waters of Baptism,
> that make an end of sin and a new beginning of goodness.

1220 If water springing up from the earth symbolises life, the water of the sea is a symbol of death and so can represent the mystery of the cross. By this symbolism Baptism signifies communion with Christ's death.

1221 But above all, the crossing of the Red Sea, literally the liberation of Israel from the slavery of Egypt, announces the liberation wrought by Baptism:

> You freed the children of Abraham from the slavery of Pharaoh,
> bringing them dry-shod through the waters of the Red Sea,
> to be an image of the people set free in Baptism.

1222 Finally, Baptism is prefigured in the crossing of the Jordan River by which the People of God received the gift of the land promised to Abraham's descendants, an image of eternal life. The promise of this blessed inheritance is fulfilled in the New Covenant.

Christ's Baptism

1223 All the Old Covenant prefigurations find their fulfilment in Christ Jesus. He begins his public life after having himself baptised by St. John the Baptist in the Jordan. After his resurrection Christ gives this mission to his apostles: 'Go therefore and make disciples of all nations, baptising them in the name of the Father and of the Son and of the Holy Spirit, teaching them to observe all that I have commanded you.'

1224 Our Lord voluntarily submitted himself to the baptism of St. John, intended for sinners, in order to 'fulfil all righteousness'. Jesus' gesture is a manifestation of his self-emptying. The Spirit who had hovered over the waters of the first creation descended then on the Christ as a prelude of the new creation, and the Father revealed Jesus as his 'beloved Son'.

1225 In his Passover Christ opened to all men the fountain of Baptism. He had already spoken of his Passion, which he was about to suffer in Jerusalem, as a 'Baptism' with which he had to be baptised. The blood and water that flowed from the pierced side of the crucified Jesus are types of Baptism and the Eucharist, the sacraments of new life. From then on, it is possible 'to be born of water and the Spirit' in order to enter the Kingdom of God.

> See where you are baptised, see where Baptism comes from, if not from the cross of Christ, from his death.
> There is the whole mystery: he died for you. In him you are redeemed, in him you are saved.

Baptism in the Church

1226 From the very day of Pentecost the Church has celebrated and administered holy Baptism. Indeed St. Peter declares to the crowd astounded by his preaching: 'Repent, and be baptised every one of you in the name of Jesus Christ for the forgiveness of your sins; and you shall receive the gift of the Holy Spirit.'

Session 6

Whose Story?

'He interpreted for them all the scriptures' (Luke 24:27)

God our Father, We heard with our own ears, we have been told the story of the things you did long ago, the wonderful deeds which you performed. Send your Spirit upon your Church and do great deeds again in our time, O Lord, so that your power and wisdom, which you revealed in Christ, may be celebrated throughout the world. Amen.

In this session we look at the Catholic Story, the History of Salvation. This is the wonderful Story in which we find our true identity. As catechists we need to know this Story well and be able to communicate it to others. It is the context within which we place our teaching on all other matters.

Tell the Story

'The Church, in transmitting today the Christian message... has a constant memory of the saving events of the past and makes them known. In the light of these, she interprets the present events of human history, where the Spirit of God is continually renewing the face of the earth, and she waits with faith for the Lord's coming.'
GDC 107

From the beginning

From the earliest times in the Church we find that an essential part of catechesis has been telling others the Story of Creation and Salvation.

Let us look at one of the first instances. We find this in the Gospel of St Luke. After the crucifixion of Jesus the disciples were devastated. The One in whom they had placed all their hopes had been cruelly killed. To whom could they now turn in order to discover meaning and joy in their lives again? In Luke 24 we find two of the disciples walking out from Jerusalem to a small village called Emmaus. On their journey they are met by a stranger who walks alongside them.

Finding faith through the Story

1. **Listen to this passage, Luke 24:13-35.**

   Notice how the two disciples are able to tell the last few days of the Story but do not have faith because they need to hear the whole of it. A small part, by itself, does not make sense to them. This whole Story is what Jesus tells them.

The Church calls this Story of Salvation the *'narratio'*, or 'narration'. It is the narrative of the Faith. What we believe is not primarily a set of timeless truths, but truths that we discover within a living history. The *General Directory for Catechesis* says that this Story, this history, read within the perspective of faith, is 'a fundamental part of the content of catechesis.' (GDC 108).

The Church's catechesis is placed within the story of salvation, the 'narratio'.

The point of the Story

This Story has love as its source, driving force, and goal.

> 'The whole concern of doctrine and its teaching must be directed to the love that never ends. Whether something is proposed for belief, for hope or for action, the love of our Lord must always be made accessible, so that anyone can see that all the works of perfect Christian virtue spring from love and have no other objective than to arrive at love' (CCC 25).

The role of the catechist, then, is to share with others the Story of God's never-ending love.

Coming to faith means coming to believe in the truth of this Story. And the Story is not outside of ourselves. It is *our* Story.

Every teaching we deliver, then, should flow from, and be directed towards, participation in the Catholic Story. For this Story includes, with the telling of it, an invitation to join the Catholic family and make the Story one's own.

The whole point of the Story, from beginning to end, is the love of God revealed in Christ.

The parts of the Story

The Story is grounded, of course, in the life of the Trinity:

> 'The whole history of salvation is identical with the history of the way and the means by which the one true God, Father, Son and Holy Spirit, reveals himself to men "and reconciles and unites with Himself those who turn away from sin" ' (CCC 234).

Like all good stories, the Catholic Story has a beginning, a middle and an end. The **beginning** is the act of Creation. The **middle** is the coming of Christ, his Incarnation, Life, death, Resurrection and Ascension. The **end** is the Second Coming of Christ, which ushers in the Final Judgement for the whole of humanity.

These give us the key marker points in the Story. They tell us where we must start and finish and where the Story reaches its central climax – in the redemptive life and work of Christ.

The *General Directory for Catechesis* describes the main sections of the Story, through which God has revealed himself to us, as:

> 'the great stages of the **Old Testament** by which God prepared the journey of the Gospel; **the life of Jesus**, Son of God, born of the Virgin Mary, who by his actions and teaching brought Revelation to completion; **the history of the Church** which transmits Revelation.' (108)

The three stages of the Story are the times of the Old Testament starting with Creation, the New Testament, and the history of the Church ending with the Second Coming.

Telling the Story

What are the main points that make up the Story? Let us look at the sections of the Story in more detail now. We can examine this unfolding of Revelation, as God reaches for us throughout Salvation History, within the overall three stages.

2 The first stage: Creation, the Fall and the Promise of Salvation

- God our uncreated Creator, is a Trinity, a family of Persons, who has a plan for us
- God created all things, visible and invisible. We emphasise the goodness of creation, humanity being created in God's image, and the creation of angels
- The Fall: sin, death, and the corruption of the human family's relationship with God. We also speak of the loss of harmony between people and between humanity and creation
- God's gathering of a people to himself: the covenants with Noah, Abraham, Moses and David as steps towards the restoration of communion
- God's promises through the Prophets of the establishing of a new relationship, a new covenant

The second stage: the Life of God the Son

- The Incarnation: Jesus is true God and true Man. This is the centre of the Story
- Mary's unique participation in God's gift of himself, her 'yes' to God, the supreme example of grace working to bring about human cooperation with God's plan
- Jesus' preaching and teaching on the Kingdom of God in which all things will be restored
- The Paschal Mystery: Jesus' Suffering, Death, Resurrection and Ascension for our redemption

- The establishing of the universal Church in which God re-gathers us again in Christ

The third stage: the Era of the Church
- The Descent of the Holy Spirit at Pentecost: he is the guarantor of the deposit of faith and the life of the deposit of grace
- The Story since Pentecost: a new family identity, the saints, all of us here and now
- Our 'waiting in joyful hope' for the coming of Christ. We live in expectation. The Church calls this part of the Story the time of the *'expectatio'*, the awaiting
- The Second Coming of Jesus and Heaven

Identifying the parts

3 Look at the Creed which we say at Mass and identify the three stages of the *narratio*, of the Catholic Story.

Now look carefully at the extract from Eucharistic Prayer 4 and find the *narratio* there.

It is important to know clearly the outline of the Story of Salvation, from beginning to end.

The Story in the Catechism

The *General Directory for Catechesis* speaks of seven 'foundation stones' or 'basic elements' which need to lie at the heart of all catechesis. We find all of them in the Catechism.

Four of these foundation stones are the four parts of the Catechism. As you know, these four parts correspond to the four dimensions of the Christian life:

- the Profession of Faith (Part 1)
- the Celebration of the Mystery (Part 2)
- Life in Christ (Part 3)
- Christian Prayer (Part 4)

These are the four pillars of the Christian life: we believe, worship, live and pray.

The other three foundation stones are 'the three phases in the narration of the history of salvation' (GDC 130): the Old Testament, the life of Jesus and the history of the Church.

The General Directory for Catechesis asks us to set our expositions of the Faith, worship life and prayer of the Church *within* this narrative framework. In other words, when we catechise and explain the truths of Catholic faith and life we are helping our hearers to understand these things as elements within a story, a story in which they share.

The Catechism and the Story

4 Look at the way in which the Catechism places its teaching on Baptism within the framework of the History of Salvation CCC 1217-1226. Other examples of how the Catechism places doctrine within the Story of Salvation are listed in the further reading.

The Catechism models for us the setting of our teaching within the narratio.

Using the Story in catechesis

Finally, let us look at some practical ideas about using the Story in our handing on of the Faith.

- Telling the Story could take just five minutes, it could take thirty minutes or it could be examined more in-depth and take as long as time allows. The way in which we tell the Story, what we select, what we omit and what we choose to emphasise, depends to a large extent on the particular situation and audience. We need to practice telling the Story in a variety of situations.
- All those whom we catechise need to know this Story and be invited to make it their own. Tell the Story using 'our', 'we' and 'us' to make it clear that it really is the Story of the Catholic 'family'.
- It is often helpful to use beautiful and striking art to illustrate and bring home the Story. Pictures can be powerful and people often remember points better once they are linked to visual images.
- The Catholic Story needs to inform all that we hand on. Repeating the Story to a group in a number of different ways can often be beneficial, reinforcing ideas for the group. Tell the Story early in your catechesis so that everything that is heard subsequently can be placed within this framework. Then tell the Story again towards the end – those you are catechising will listen to the Story with new knowledge and understanding.
- Remember the overall purpose of telling the Story – to open us to the love and grace of God so that we can share in his life and love, see what is involved in becoming perfect in love as the 'heavenly Father is perfect' (Matt 5:48) and come to the glory of the Trinity. By keeping the purpose of the Story in mind, each truth we learn becomes an episode in the continuing Story of God's love for us.

We learn the Story well so that we can tell it in a number of different ways.

Summary

In this fifth session we have been looking at:

- **The Catholic Story, the History of Salvation.**
- **The main parts of this Story and the key teaching points we need to emphasise.**
- **The Story as it is presented in the Scriptures and the Catechism.**
- **Why we need to know this Story well and place our teaching within this History of Salvation.**
- **The fact that we need to invite those we are catechising to make this Story the one in which they, too, find their identity.**
- **The love of the Holy Trinity as the source and goal of all things.**

Further reading

- CCC 54-67 sets out the basic salvation history. The Scriptural verses referred to here are helpful for developing the outline of the story.
- Psalms 105 and 136 are examples of early recountings of the story in the Old Testament.
- The Benedictus (Luke 1:67-79) and the speech of the first martyr, Stephen (Acts 7:2-53) are examples of New Testament tellings of the story.
- Other examples from the Catechism where doctrine is placed within the Story of Salvation are: The Church (CCC 758-769), The Holy Spirit (CCC 702-741) and The Eucharist (CCC 1333-1344).

Glossary on the Story

Covenant: *spousal promise of faithfulness.*

Narratio: *the narrative, or Story, of our salvation*

Expectatio: *the period in which we now live as we await the second coming of Christ.*

Catholic: *universal, whole; the Catholic Story is the whole story for all to join, from Adam to the last human being.*

Final meditation and prayer

Mary, you stand at the heart of God's plan for our salvation. Because of your 'yes' to God, the Word was made flesh and came to dwell among us. You live now in the glory of the Holy Trinity. Pray for us, that we may come to share in that same glory and know the fulfilment of God's plan for our lives. We ask this in the name of your Son, Jesus Christ, our Lord. Amen.

Leading Session 7 – Who Are We?

Preparation

- **Read** through session 7 carefully yourself, together with these notes, before the session. Think about which sections you will ask participants to read. Practise the pronunciation of Latin-based words if you are not sure of them.

- Bring to the session pens, pencils, some paper, and a copy of a Bible.

- Prepare the room to provide a prayerful and welcoming atmosphere. Get refreshments ready.

The main activity in this session needs careful preparation. This is the filling in of the chart on page three of the studysheet. To prepare for this read through handout 1 which is the same chart correctly completed.

You will see that there are two exercises here. The first one is to write which office of the Church and ministry of Christ is being exercised.

The second exercise is about participation. For this there are 4 ways of filling in the spaces, that is, four ways of ticking 'yes' to participation. You may prefer to suggest that people just put a tick or a cross and you explain afterwards from the handout the different requirements for participation indicated by the four symbols. Decide beforehand which method will suit your group best.

This exercise is likely to stimulate considerable discussion. The handout of the completed list will help here. It may help to know that the completed list reflects the requirements of the office and ministry as laid down by the Church in her teaching; it might not be the same as common practice.

Photocopy sufficient numbers of the handout and give it out at the end of the exercise to help in the discussion that will follow. The answers are given in this handout to prevent confusion.

At the session

Have the title and Scripture passage read out aloud and then *pray* together.
Introduce the session.

Stop at the numbered dot

❶ Explain the six columns in the activity and what participants are expected to do in each column. You may wish to separate it into two activities.

You could lead the filling in of the first two columns as a whole group exercise, especially as the two columns go together – in other words, once it is seen, for example, that the role is one of *'sanctifying'* then it will also always be the ministry of *'priest'*.

You could then ask members of your group to work in twos and threes to fill in the remaining columns. Ask them to indicate what they think it should be and then we will discuss afterwards. It is not meant to be a test. The group will be familiar with the action list after discussing it together for the first exercise.

Conclude with the summary and say together the *final prayer*.

Echoes Session 7 Handout 1

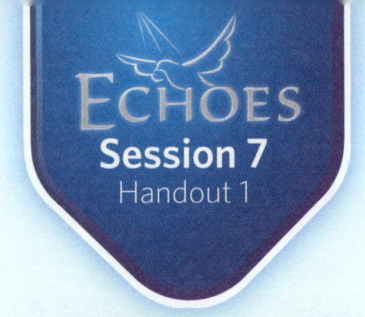

CHRIST'S THREEFOLD MINISTRY OF PROPHET, PRIEST AND KING

As exercised in the three offices of the Church – Teaching, Sanctifying and Governing

Action	Office of the Church	Ministry of Christ	Bishop	Priest	Deacon	Lay Person
To own church property	Governing	King	■			
To make legal decisions	Governing	King	■	■		
To decide parish policy	Governing	King	■	■		
To preside at Mass	All Three	All Three	■	■		
To proclaim the Gospel at Mass	Teaching	Prophet	■	■	■	
To proclaim a homily at Mass	Teaching	Prophet	■	■		
To preach at any other time or occasion	Teaching	Prophet	■	■	■	●
To read the First and Second Readings	Teaching	Prophet	■	■	■	▶
To read the Bidding Prayers	Sanctifying	Priest	▲	■	■	■
To distribute Holy Communion	Sanctifying	Priest	■	■	■	●
To prepare someone for Baptism	Teaching	Prophet	■	■	■	▶
To preside at the Sacrament of Baptism	All Three	All Three	■	■	■	●
To preside at the Sacrament of Confirmation	All Three	All Three	■	▲		
To prepare someone for the Sacrament of Marriage	Teaching	Prophet	■	■	■	▶
To preside at Sacrament of Holy Orders	All Three	All Three	■			
To preside at the Sacrament of the Sick	All Three	All Three	■	■		
To give Communion to the sick and housebound	Sanctifying	Priest	■	■	■	●
To prepare for the Sacrament of Reconciliation	Teaching	Prophet	■	■	■	▶
To preside at the Sacramant of Reconciliation	All Three	All Three	■	■		
To administer a funeral service, burial or cremation	Sanctifying	Priest	■	■	■	●
To prepare someone for the Sacrament of the Eucharist	Teaching	Prophet	■	■	■	▶
To expose the Blessed Sacrament with Benediction	Sanctifying	Priest	■	■	■	
To expose the Blessed Sacrament with simple Exposition	Sanctifying	Priest	■	■	■	●
To lead the Stations of the Cross	Sanctifying	Priest	■	■	■	■
To lead Morning and Evening Prayer	Sanctifying	Priest	■	■	■	■
To participate in the offertory procession	Sanctifying	Priest	▲	▲	▲	■
To lead or help with the Children's Liturgy	Teaching	Prophet	▲	▲	■	▶
To serve at the altar	Sanctifying	Priest	▲	▲	■	▶
To prepare the parish newsletter	Governing	King	▲	■	■	■
To clean or help maintain the church building and grounds	Governing	King	▲	▲	■	■
To arrange flowers in the church	Governing	King	▲	▲	■	■
To lead or help with RCIA	Teaching	Prophet	▲	■	■	▶

- ■ participates in the ministry of Christ expressed in the offices of the Church
- ▶ participates usually as part of a parish team and with training
- ● may participate in extraordinary circumstances and with training
- ▲ may participate in this way but it would be unusual

Session 7

Who are we?

'You shall be consecrated to me'
Exodus 22:31

God our Saviour,
Through the grace of Baptism you made us children of light sharing in the mission of your beloved Son.
Hear our prayer that we may always walk in that light and work for truth as your witnesses. We ask this in the name of Jesus your Son, Amen.

In the last session, we were looking at our Story, the Story which we join by Baptism into Christ, and it is in virtue of our rebirth **in Christ** that we also share Christ's mission. Christ's mission is described from the earliest times as that of Priest, Prophet and King. In this session we answer the question, 'who are we?' by exploring what it means for us, in the Church, to be Priest, Prophet and King in Christ.

In the Church this mission is shared by the clergy and the lay faithful in different but complementary ways, 'for in the Church there is diversity of ministry but unity of mission' (CCC 873). We will therefore need to look at who we are in relation to the ordained ministers especially the parish priest and permanent deacons.

> 'Jesus Christ is the one whom the Father anointed with the Holy Spirit and established as priest, prophet and king. The whole People of God participates in these three offices of Christ and bears the responsibilities for mission and service that flow from them.' (CCC 783)

Priest, Prophet and King

The word 'Christ' comes from the Hebrew word meaning 'anointed'. In the Old Testament we find three types of people who were anointed which meant that they were consecrated or set apart to help in God's mission. The three types of people were prophets, priests and kings and so Christ, as the perfect one fulfilling God's mission completely, is understood by the Church as *perfect* Priest, *perfect* Prophet and *perfect* King.

Christ's mission, then, from the earliest times, has been understood as a unity of these three roles. These three roles sum up his mission. They are also united in his body, the Church, and sum up the Church's mission.

- The priest makes sacrifices and offers worship to God – in the Church this is called the sanctifying office.
- The prophet is one who proclaims or teaches the Word of God – in the Church this is called the teaching office.
- The king directs the lives of the people in accordance with God's laws – in the Church this is called the governing office.

We will consider what sharing in Christ's priestly, prophetic and royal office means for us in practice. Firstly, however, we will look at these offices in the light of the diversity of ministry that exists in the Church.

The roles of priest, prophet and king sum up Christ's and the Church's mission.

Common Priesthood of the faithful and the Ministerial Priesthood

There is a very important sentence from the Council document *Lumen gentium*, for understanding the difference between those who are ordained (permanent deacons, priests, bishops) and those who are lay people (parents, catechists etc.). The common priesthood of

(65)

the faithful and the ministerial priesthood (ordained) 'though they differ essentially and not only in degree... are none the less ordered one to another; [since] each in its own proper way shares in the one priesthood of Christ' (LG 10).

The **ministerial priesthood** is at the service of the **common priesthood** that we all share. The ministerial priesthood 'ministers', that is, it serves, supports, leads, governs, teaches, builds and nourishes the common priesthood of all the faithful. Without the ministerial priesthood, without that 'sacred ministering', the common priesthood cannot function properly. Without lay participation, the ministerial priesthood does not function properly either.

'The ministerial priesthood is a means by which Christ unceasingly builds up and leads his Church. For this reason it is transmitted by its own sacrament, the Sacrament of Holy Orders' (CCC 1547).

The common priesthood and ministerial priesthood share in different ways in the one priesthood of Christ.

The mission of the laity

The Fathers of The Second Vatican Council developed a vision of the laity as those who can permeate the secular world with the Spirit of Christ. This is possible through bearing witness in their personal, family and social lives by proclaiming and sharing the gospel of Christ in the situations in which they find themselves, and by their involvement with the task of explaining, defending, and applying Christian principles to the problems of today's world.

In addition to this, the lay faithful may be called to *assist* in the sacred ministry of the clergy (especially as readers, catechists and extraordinary ministers of Holy Communion). Since these tasks are most closely linked to the duties of pastors, that is, ordained ministers, it is necessary to remember:

- that the ordained minister (usually a priest, sometimes a deacon) remains ultimately responsible in these areas
- that 'collaboration with' the priest does not mean 'substitution for' him
- that care should be taken to safeguard the nature and mission of sacred ministry
- that care should be taken to safeguard the vocation and proper character of the lay faithful
- that the training received by the priest over many years is an indication of the seriousness of the ministry in the eyes of the Church reminding lay people that training is absolutely essential for them too
- that lay participation here is to a limited degree and in a prescribed manner.

Because many dioceses are looking to the laity to provide increased assistance in parishes, it may be helpful to look at the role of the parish and the parish priest before we consider lay participation in Christ's priestly, prophetic and royal office.

Lay people have their own proper calling and can also assist in the sacred ministry.

The Parish and the Parish Priest

In general, the parish is the local manifestation of the universal Church. The Code of Canon Law defines the parish as: 'A certain community of Christ's faithful ... whose pastoral care, under the authority of the diocesan bishop, is entrusted to its parish priest as its proper pastor' (canon 515).

The parish priest is the proper pastor of the parish entrusted to him, under the diocesan bishop, so that for his community he may carry out the offices of sanctifying, teaching and ruling with the co-operation of other priests and deacons and with the assistance of lay members in accordance with the law (see canon 519).

1 Fill in the chart below with what you think they should be be. In the first two columns write in the ministry and office. In the next 4 columns write in the type of participation using one of the 4 symbols. 3 are filled in to help you get started.

CHRIST'S THREEFOLD MINISTRY OF PROPHET, PRIEST AND KING
As exercised in the three offices of the Church — Teaching, Sanctifying and Governing

Action	Office of the Church	Ministry of Christ	Bishop	Priest	Deacon	Lay Person
To own church property						
To make legal decisions						
To decide parish policy	Governing	King	■	■		
To preside at Mass						
To proclaim the Gospel at Mass	Teaching	Prophet	■	■	■	
To proclaim a homily at Mass						
To preach at any other time or occasion						
To read the First and Second Readings						
To read the Bidding Prayers						
To distribute Holy Communion						
To prepare someone for Baptism						
To preside at the Sacrament of Baptism	All Three	All Three	■	■	■	●
To preside at the Sacrament of Confirmation						
To prepare someone for the Sacrament of Marriage						
To preside at Sacrament of Holy Orders						
To preside at the Sacrament of the Sick						
To give Communion to the sick and housebound						
To prepare for the Sacrament of Reconciliation						
To preside at the Sacramant of Reconciliation						
To administer a funeral service, burial or cremation						
To prepare someone for the Sacrament of the Eucharist						
To expose the Blessed Sacrament with Benediction						
To expose the Blessed Sacrament with simple Exposition						
To lead the Stations of the Cross						
To lead Morning and Evening Prayer						
To participate in the offertory procession						
To lead or help with the Children's Liturgy						
To serve at the altar						
To prepare the parish newsletter						
To clean or help maintain the church building and grounds						
To arrange flowers in the church						
To lead or help with RCIA						

■ participates in the ministry of Christ expressed in the offices of the Church
▶ participates usually as part of a parish team and with training
● may participate in extraordinary circumstances and with training
▲ may participate in this way but it would be unusual

Canon Law also establishes a parish as a juridical person (canon 515). In other words the 'parish' is the person responsible in law, which means that the people in the parish are not subject to legal rights and obligations, the 'parish' is. It is the parish priest who represents the parish.

The collaboration of the faithful with the priest in his pastoral ministry should lead to an enrichment of the Church but it is necessary to have a clear understanding of both the non-ordained and ordained person's participation in Christ's mission in order to achieve a harmonious, working relationship which results in the building up of the Church.

Clarity about roles and responsibilities is vital for fruitful catechesis in the parish.

Summary:

In this session we have looked at:

- **The participation of the laity in the three offices of Christ: Priest, Prophet and King.**
- **An explanation of the common priesthood of the faithful and the ministerial priesthood.**
- **The nature of the parish and the role of the Parish Priest.**
- **How the laity can assist the priest in his Sacred Ministry.**

Further Reading

- GDC 230-232: the roles of the lay catechist explained.
- CCC 888-896: covers the teaching, sanctifying and governing offices in the Church.
- CCC 897-900: the Church's teaching on the laity.
- CCC 901 to 913: what it means for the laity to participate in Christ's mission.

Glossary of words associated with Parish Mission

Mission: *from the Latin word 'missio' meaning 'I send'. 'Mission' is what Christ and the Church are sent by God the Father to do, in the power of the Holy Spirit. We share the one mission of the Trinity.*

Ministry: *from the Latin word 'munus' meaning 'service'. 'Sacred Ministry' is the title given to the service of ordained ministers because of the sacred power by which they act.*

Office: *a function or position in the Church founded in either divine or Church law and exercised for a spiritual purpose.*

Pastor, Pastoral: *'pastor' comes from the Latin word for shepherd. A shepherd guards over and leads the flock, and so pastoral ministry is similar to the kingly office of Christ. Christ lives his kingship as a good shepherd.*

Juridical person: *the one responsible before the law. The one responsible does not have to be an individual human person but can be a group (like school governors), or a group that is represented by someone, as a parish is by the parish priest.*

Code of Canon Law: *The Code of Canon Law is a book of regulations drawn from the life of the Church and is written to make clear the roles and responsibilities necessary in the Spirit-filled life of the Church.*

Closing Prayer

Holy Spirit, fill our hearts that they may grow in your gifts enabling us to develop our full potential in this life. May we be filled with your abundance and love, finding fulfilment and happiness whilst seeking always the values of the Gospel and the well being of others. Amen.

Leading Session 8: Why link with the Liturgy?

Preparation
- Read through session 8 carefully yourself, together with these notes, before the session. Check particularly that you understand the activities.
- Think about which sections you will ask participants to read.
- Practise the pronunciation of Latin-based words if you are not sure.
- There are no handouts for this session.
- Prepare the room to provide a prayerful and welcoming atmosphere.
- Get refreshments ready.
- Bring to the session pens, pencils, some paper, a copy of a Bible, and a Catechism. It would help to bring a Catholic diary, the Diocesan Directory, or a copy of Morning and Evening prayer, in order to show the kinds of liturgical information available from various sources.

At the session
Read the title, followed by the sentence from Scripture, and then *pray*.
Then read the introductory paragraph or summarise it in your own words.

Stop at the numbered dots

❶ Members of the group will have many ideas about this. On the one hand, one can make links by teaching about the liturgical year and the feasts and seasons in one's sessions. On the other hand, if one is planning a catechetical session, it is a good idea to look to the current liturgical time and use these themes in planning. You can use prayers and information given in both the Sunday and weekday missals, as well as the prayers in the Office, especially Morning and Evening prayer. You can also use information given in the diocesan directory. By linking to the liturgical time or season, you will have an increased impact on people's understanding as their understanding of the faith given in the catechetical sessions will be reinforced in and through the liturgy.

❷ Again, there will be many suggestions. The most obvious are The Sign of the Cross, The *Confiteor*, the Gloria, the Creed, the *Sanctus*, the Our Father, the *Agnus dei*, and the dialogue parts of the Mass. One might also mention the three canticles from the Office: the *Benedictus* from Morning Prayer, the *Magnificat* from Evening Prayer and the *Nunc Dimittis* from Night Prayer.

❸ Some suggestions here would be:
- the gathering of the assembly
- anointing
- the movements of the priest's hands during the Eucharistic prayer, invoking the Holy Spirit and during the consecration in particular
- kneeling
- standing
- positions of the hands in prayer
- rings in marriage
- the laying on of hands

❹ You might decide to lead a brief discussion on ways of using the liturgical colour of the season when preparing a room or environment for catechesis, for altars in the home and so on. Here are some points about the colours as background information.

Green: used in Ordinary Time. Represents virtue and hope of eternal light. You will see this colour used for a large part of the Church's Year. It is the colour of nature and the Spring to remind us that we are always being given new life throughout the Church's Year as we listen to God's Word and receive the Lord at Mass.

White: used for solemnities: important feasts, including Christmas and Easter. A sign of celebration and joy.

Red: used for feast days. Red is used at Pentecost to remind us of the fire of the Holy Spirit. Palm Sunday, Good Friday, and other feasts relating to the Holy Cross. It is also used for feasts of martyrs because they shed their blood for Christ.

Purple: for penitence. A sign of preparation. Used during Lent (before Easter) and Advent (before Christmas), in preparation for these great feasts. From the Fifth Sunday of Lent, crucifixes and statues may be draped with purple. This is to remind us that we are entering a sombre and solemn time. Crucifixes are uncovered again at the end of Good Friday and statues unveiled before the Easter Vigil in readiness for Easter.

Rose: signifies rejoicing, joy. May be used on the third Sunday of Advent, and the Fourth Sunday of Lent, to show that, as well as the solemn time of preparation, we are looking forward to a time of rejoicing and joy.

Black: signifies the sorrow of death and the darkness of the Lamb.

Read the *summary* to sum up the session.

Point out, once again, that the *further reading* is optional. People might also be invited to spend time familiarizing themselves with a missal, especially with the feasts and seasons.

Say together the *final prayer*.

In time relaxing after the session you might look informally at Catholic diaries, the diocesan directory, or a copy of Morning and Evening prayer, in order to see what kinds of liturgical information is available from various sources.

Session 8

Why link with the liturgy?

Christ, our spiritual and eternal sacrifice (Cf. Heb 9:14)

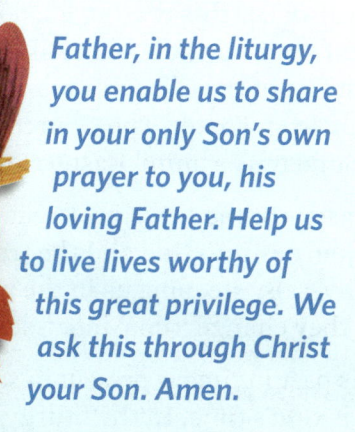

Father, in the liturgy, you enable us to share in your only Son's own prayer to you, his loving Father. Help us to live lives worthy of this great privilege. We ask this through Christ your Son. Amen.

In this session we look first of all at why we should link catechesis with the liturgy. We also consider what liturgy is and examine some of the key elements of liturgy which are important for our catechesis. Finally, we look at three practical ways of making our catechesis liturgical.

The reasons

For the Catholic Church 'every liturgical celebration, because it is an action of Christ the priest and of his body, which is the Church, is a sacred action surpassing all others' (SC7).

We need to consider this striking statement from the Second Vatican Council's teaching on the liturgy, *Sacrosanctum concilium* (SC), very carefully. We can see from the statement that liturgy is not just the Catholic way of organising a weekly religious service of prayer. Liturgy is called a 'sacred action' and one which 'surpasses' all others. You will already have an idea of what liturgy is, so, before we look at this in more detail, let us consider a brief initial answer to the question being asked in this session.

In our catechesis we link to liturgy for three main reasons:

- Firstly, catechesis needs to be **about the liturgy**, since it is important for everyone to know what is happening in liturgical celebrations, sacred actions surpassing all others.

So, we need to be able to say what the priest and people do and why they do it, what the symbols and actions in liturgy are and what they signify.

- Secondly, all catechesis is to **lead people to participation in the liturgy** because the liturgy is the summit towards which all the activity of the Church is directed and the fount from which all her power flows (SC10).

So, we need to be able to say when the feasts and great celebrations of the liturgical year are and help others to be prepared for them.

- Thirdly, **the liturgy itself is catechesis** in its most profound form. The liturgy teaches by experience and gives what it teaches. It not only presents the mystery of Christ sacramentally, it also lets us immediately partake of his mystery.

So, we need to invite people to liturgy in the parish. We can know that bringing people into the liturgy is equivalent to bringing them into the presence of Christ.

We will look at the main points of each of these links with the liturgy but firstly let us look in more detail about what liturgy is.

It is essential that our catechesis be liturgical.

What is liturgy?

Liturgy is the public participation of the people of God in the work of God (see CCC 1069).

Many have a very limited view of liturgy as simply rules and regulations (the rubrics) which are connected to each of the celebrations of the Church's sacraments. But the Church's own understanding of liturgy, as we have seen, is that it is 'an action surpassing all others'. Liturgy is actually about the Trinity's work of Redemption and how this is communicated to the world today.

The liturgy is the worship which the Church renders to the Father through Jesus our High Priest, in the unity of the Holy Spirit. It is the worship offered by the mystical body of Christ, head and members – that is, Christ and his people.

Liturgy, then, is the communal prayer of the 'whole Christ'. Liturgy includes:

- the Eucharist, the highest form of liturgy
- the liturgy of the other sacraments
- the 'Liturgy of the Hours', or the 'Divine Office'. This is the name given to the official daily Prayer of the Church. It is largely composed of the Psalms, together with other scriptural and spiritual readings
- the Liturgy of Benediction.

We need to remember, then, that liturgy is first and foremost God's work, in and with and through his people gathered together. God comes among his people to bless them and to share his grace. Liturgy is at the heart of all Catholic life, the life of a people united with God in worship and praise.

Liturgy is our participation in the redemptive work of God.

In more detail

Let us look at five aspects of liturgy that are always important.

1. The Liturgical Year

The liturgy of the Eucharist and the Divine Office are organised each year principally around the life of Christ, from conception and birth, Baptism, temptation and Transfiguration, to Death, Resurrection and Ascension. This is called 'the Liturgical Year'. Within this cycle we also celebrate Our Lady, the apostles and the saints – some of the members of Christ's family, of *our* family in Christ.

The Liturgical year starts on the first Sunday of Advent. During the course of the year, Catholics follow, day by day, week by week, and by means of liturgical seasons and festivals, the story of salvation history, 'the Story' which we looked at in a previous session. The readings, hymns and prayers are arranged so that the story of Christ's work of redemption is unfolded like the chapters of a book.

At the heart of the Liturgical year is the Lord's resurrection. This stands at the centre of the faith, and therefore of the liturgy also. For this reason, Easter is the crown of the Liturgical year. All the other celebrations of the Church's year draw their meaning from Easter. The Church thinks of every Sunday as a 'mini' Easter Sunday.

The seasons of the Liturgical Year support us in our journey into God and the transformation of our lives. By steeping us in the mysteries of Christ they change 'time' into 'sacred time'.

What is past in time is *present* in sacred time, which is God's time. In the liturgy, what is past is made present. The Church teaches us that every day is the 'today' of God. This belief is reflected in the prayers of the liturgy. So, for example, a prayer for the day of Pentecost says, '*This* is the day of Pentecost, alleluia. *Today* the Holy Spirit appeared to the disciples in the form of fire and gave them his special gifts ..' (Magnificat antiphon, Evening Prayer II, Pentecost; *italics added*).

❶ Can you think of examples of how to link catechetical sessions to the Liturgical Year?

Arranging catechesis around the Liturgical Year is a way of sharing in the life of Christ in his Church and coming closer to him.

2. Prayer and liturgy

In the liturgy we are privileged to join with Christ in his act of love and self-offering to the Father. Liturgical prayers are the prayers of Christ the head united to his body, the Church. They are:

- prayers in the liturgy to God the Father led by the priest, who represents Christ, the Son of God
- prayers spoken or sung by the priest and people together, or in dialogue.

❷ **Can you think of examples of liturgical prayers that everyone would benefit from knowing by heart?**

Include liturgical prayers in catechesis. Explain them, learn them by heart and pray them together.

3. Liturgical signs and symbols

The liturgy is more than prayers. Just as human languages include physical signs and gestures, so the Church's liturgical language includes signs such as the bread and wine which will become the Body and Blood of Christ, symbolic materials such as water and oil, and gestures such as genuflecting, processing, and the Sign of the Cross. These signs, actions and symbols are powerful non-verbal forms of catechesis.

❸ **Can you think of other examples of signs, gestures and symbols that could be explained?**

In catechesis we can explain the meanings of the signs and symbols so that they can be experienced more fully.

4. Liturgical readings

Liturgical readings are always taken from the Scriptures in the Mass and other Sacraments, and from Scripture and Tradition in the Divine Office. The Church has brought together a wide selection of carefully-chosen readings from the whole Bible for the yearly cycle: the book of this collection is called the Lectionary (from the Latin word *'lectio'* which means 'I read'). Mass readings are always to be taken from here.

Catechesis that uses the liturgical readings helps to insert people into the liturgy where we listen to the Word of God.

5. Liturgical colours

Colour coding is used frequently in the secular world to help instant recognition in various circumstances. Think, for example, of the use of blue for 'cold' and red for 'stop, danger, hot'. The Church has her own method of colour coding according to the liturgical season and feast day, to help us to identify with the Mysteries of Christ in his Church.

❹ *It is good to know and use the liturgical colours as part of one's way of catechising.*

Liturgical catechesis

The Church 'ardently desires that all the Christian faithful be brought to that full, conscious and active participation which is required by the very nature of the liturgy and the dignity of the baptismal priesthood' (GDC 85).

Now that we have looked at what liturgy is and some of its elements, we can examine more fully what our catechesis might include for it to be liturgical.

Linked to liturgy in its content

We can teach carefully and fully about the liturgy.

> 'Liturgical catechesis aims to initiate people into the mystery of Christ by proceeding from the visible to the invisible, from the sign to the thing signified, from the Sacraments to the mysteries' (CCC 1075).

Linked to liturgy in its spirit

Our catechesis can be informed with a 'liturgical spirit', so that we are continually leading people to the liturgy of the Church where they will be able to receive Christ.

For this reason catechesis, as well as developing knowledge and understanding of the liturgy and the sacraments, must also educate the disciples of Jesus Christ in an attitude of loving respect

- for prayer - private and public
- for thanksgiving
- for repentance
- for confidence in prayer
- for community spirit

since all of this 'is necessary for a true liturgical life' (see GDC 85).

Linked to liturgy in its planning
Planning has to do with the use of time. God created time for the same reason that he created everything else: so that he could use it to lead us to salvation. We can plan our catechesis carefully so that our topics link to the Liturgical year and encourage participation in the Church's liturgy.

In this way our catechesis is linked to sacred time.

To help you, it is a good idea to use a Catholic diary. This will have all the dates of the Church's Liturgical Year, its seasons and feast days. (The Diocesan Directory or Diocesan *Ordo* will also have the special feast days and the liturgical colours for your particular diocese). By noting these as you plan catechetical sessions you are already beginning to see time in a sacred way, to see time as the Church sees it, and to link sessions to seasons and liturgical celebrations. Such planning builds the parish as a worshipping community.

Summary

In this eighth session we have been considering:

- **why catechesis needs to be liturgical.**
- **what liturgy is and what are some of its important elements for catechesis.**
- **three practical ways of making catechesis more liturgical.**

Further Reading

- CCC 1066-1075: the Catechism explains the basics about the liturgy and the importance of liturgical catechesis.
- CCC 1163-1173: the liturgical year explained.

Glossary on the Liturgy

Sacrosanctum concilium (SC): *the document from the Second Vatican Council on the Liturgy.*

Redemption: *the work of the Holy Trinity saving us through the Life, Death and Resurrection of Christ. This work of Redemption is made present to us, and 'applied' to us, in the sacrifice of the Mass.*

Benediction: *A time of adoration of the Blessed Sacrament outside of the Mass which concludes with the blessing (benediction) of those present.*

Lectionary: *the Cycle of Readings chosen to accompany the Mass. The Sunday readings are organized around a three-year cycle: Year A (St Matthew), Year B (St Mark) and Year C (St Luke). Parts of St John are read during each year. The weekday readings are organized around a two-year cycle.*

Sacred time: *God's time, into which we enter in the liturgy. What is past in time is made present in God's time.*

Signs and symbols: *physical realities through which we communicate with other people and with God.*

Final Prayer

*Almighty and everliving God,
by whose Spirit the whole body of the Church is governed and sanctified:
hear our prayer which we offer for all your faithful people, that each in his vocation and ministry may serve you in holiness and truth to the glory of your Name.
We ask this through Christ our Lord.
Amen.*

Leading Session 9 – What is the Mystery?

Preparation
- Read through these session 9 notes carefully and the studysheet itself.
- There are no handouts for this session but there will be quite a lot of reflection on the particular parish situation.
- Think about which sections you will ask participants to read.
- Practise the pronunciation of Latin-based words if you are not sure.
- Bring to the session pens: pencils, some paper, a copy of a Bible, and a copy of the Catechism.
- Prepare the room to provide a prayerful and welcoming atmosphere.
- Get refreshments ready.

At the Session
Read the title, followed by the sentence from Scripture, and then *pray*.

Then read the introductory paragraph or summarise it in your own words to introduce the session.

Stop at the numbered dots

❶ Read out the activity and wait for people to respond. Guide them to the text if they do not find it for themselves.

What is the mystery?
It is described here as having been revealed as God's plan of loving goodness, formed from all eternity in Christ.

Why did God reveal his mystery?
He revealed his plan of love through an utterly free decision for the benefit of all the people of the earth.

How did he reveal his mystery?
He revealed his mystery 'by sending us his beloved Son, our Lord Jesus Christ, and the Holy Spirit'.

❷ Read out the activity and wait for people to respond. Again, lead them towards one or two ideas to get them started if necessary.

Examples which indicate the sacredness of the altar would be:

- The priest kisses the altar when he enters onto the sanctuary and leaves it.
- The faithful bow towards the altar when approaching it in the liturgy.
- At some Masses the altar is incensed to indicate its sacredness.
- Cloths always cover the altar.
- Flowers are often placed at the base of the altar.
- Some churches have statues of angels bending in adoration towards the altar and what takes place upon it.

(Remember that genuflection is reserved as reverence for the Blessed Sacrament in the tabernacle rather than for the altar)

❸ Stop for a few minutes to discuss this. Some find it hard to imagine but that does not mean it is not true. The angels and saints are present with us in some sense, even if we can't see or feel them. How the sanctuary looks can help to remind us, and can increase or decrease the sense, that something sacred and heavenly is taking place. Some hymns can help us appreciate this more too.

❹ How do we show respect for the Lectern, the readings and the gospel? Suggestions will come from the group. Some suggestions might be as follows: (Remember that some children and teenagers need to be taught these things and why they are done)

- The lectern and the altar might have matching cloths
- The lectern can be kept clean and uncluttered
- Respectful dress chosen for presenting the Word of God to the people
- Respectful approach to the lectern by the readers
- By singing Alleluia before the Gospel is read
- By incensing the Gospel book
- Respect is also shown by quiet attention

Conclude with the *summary*.

Say together the concluding *prayer*.

Session 9

What is the Mystery?

'Worship the Father in Spirit and in Truth' (Jn 4:23)

Come, Lord Jesus! Come in the sacraments and liturgy, come in our lives, and come in Your heavenly glory! Amen.

In this session our topic is the Mystery, the mystery of the life of God himself, the life of the Blessed Trinity. It includes God's plan of unfathomable love for us, a plan for our good, our salvation through Christ. In its fullest sacramental form the mystery is made present for us in the Mass. Here, we look at how this Mystery of love is the source and purpose of the liturgy and also the source and purpose of our catechesis. All catechesis is given in order to insert us more fully into the Mystery.

The Mystery

The Church uses the word 'mystery' in a very particular way in liturgy. 'Mystery' is always:

- **divine** and therefore it is always above and beyond us. But it is also
- **revealed** and therefore it is knowable by us to some extent. What we know from revelation is true but always known in a limited way. We can know truly about God's mystery but never know fully.
- **merciful** love. God always reveals his divine mystery as merciful and loving.

God's mystery is revealed as the merciful plan of the Trinity, a plan of unfathomable love.

> 'By natural reason man can know God with certainty, on the basis of his works. But there is another order of knowledge, which man cannot possibly arrive at by his own powers: the order of divine Revelation. Through an utterly free decision, God has revealed himself and given himself to man. This he does by revealing the mystery, his plan of loving goodness, formed from all eternity in Christ, for the benefit of all men. God has fully revealed this plan by sending us his beloved Son, our Lord Jesus Christ, and the Holy Spirit.' (CCC 50)

1 From your reading of this quotation:

what is the mystery?

why did God reveal it?

how did God reveal it?

So, when we read or hear phrases with another word attached to 'mystery', such as 'Paschal Mystery', we must remember that this is the divine, merciful love of God that is revealed in something to us so that we can get a glimpse of something far beyond us. (In the case of the Paschal Mystery it is revealed in Jesus' Passion, death, Resurrection and Ascension.)

Mystery is God's infinite love revealed and made visible.

Catechesis and the mystery

In catechesis we speak about the mystery of God, of all that God has revealed to us in Christ. As we do so we remember that the full reality of Christ and of God always lies far beyond what we can understand or communicate. And so we catechise with a profound sense of awe and reverence before the mystery we proclaim.

We saw in the last session that the liturgy actually gives, makes present, the mystery about which we teach. The Catechism speaks of the time since Pentecost as that of the 'dispensation of the mystery' – in other words, the time during which 'Christ manifests, makes present and communicates his work of salvation through the liturgy of his Church' (CCC 1076). During this time the Lord acts through the sacraments: they make present for us the Redemption which he has won. Because of this, the Catechism describes the sacraments and liturgy as the 'privileged place' for catechising the People of God.

Our catechesis should lead people into the presence of the mystery.

The centre of the mystery

The centre of the mystery is God's infinite love made present for us. This revelation and making present takes place in a manner surpassing all others in the Eucharist. The Second Vatican Council calls the Eucharist 'the source and summit of the Christian life' (LG 11) and the Catechism describes the Eucharist as 'the sum and summary of our faith' (CCC 1327).

We will therefore examine aspects of the Eucharist and its celebration. Reflecting upon these will guide us in our catechesis so that it truly leads others to a deeper participation in the Mystery.

By 'participation' the Church does not mean 'as much outward activity as possible', but, rather, an inward involvement, by attentiveness to, and faith in, what is happening in the liturgy.

Our catechesis is to be orientated towards a deep participation in the Eucharist.

Worship: our response to the Sacred Mystery

We saw in the last session that the Holy Trinity is at work in the liturgy. In the liturgy the mystery of God is revealed to our minds and our senses. We see the Father, the Son and the Holy Spirit at work for our redemption. The centre of this work is the Eucharist.

In the Eucharist we share in the worship which the Church renders to the Father through Jesus our High Priest, by the power of the Holy Spirit.

Faced with the mystery, our response is worship. This is the approach we take to God who reveals himself. What he reveals evokes praise, thanksgiving, reverence and awe.

Worship is our response to the mystery.

The church building for the sacred mystery

We must remember that the interior of a church is not just a container to be filled as we like. The Catechism defines a church as:

> 'a house of prayer in which the Eucharist is celebrated and reserved, where the faithful assemble, and where is worshipped the presence of the Son of God our Saviour, offered for us on the sacrificial altar for the help and consolation of the faithful – this house ought to be in good taste and a worthy place for prayer and sacred ceremonial. In this 'house of God' the truth and the harmony of the signs that make it up should show Christ to be present and active in this place.' (CCC 1181)

The church is built up from its centre, its heart, which is the altar. The altar is the place where the sacrifice of the Cross is made present. Closely connected to this is the tabernacle where Christ may be continually adored. Nearby is the lectern from which Christ's Word is proclaimed. Christ in his paschal mystery, then, is the central point in every church, and it is around him that the congregation assembles, building up the Body of Christ and centring all our worship of God around the altar.

Explaining these points helps to provide an answer to those who ask why we need to go to a church to worship.

❷ Can you think of actions which indicate the sacredness of the altar?

Awareness of the mystery will enable us to recover a 'sense of the sacred' in all that surrounds our worship. He is with us!

Sharing in the mystery of heaven

Christian worship is earthly, using the things of this world and all natural, human talents. At the same time it is heavenly because it brings us into the presence of God. When we on earth celebrate the liturgy, especially the liturgy of the Mass. We sing the Holy, Holy, Holy Lord with the whole Church in heaven. We offer the Eucharistic sacrifice with Mary, the Mother of God and with all the saints. In our small parish church we are united to heaven.

3 *How aware are we that the earthly liturgy we celebrate in our parishes is participation in the liturgy of heaven?*

The Eucharist is celebrated by the 'whole Christ', head and body, that is with all the saints and angels in the heavenly kingdom.

Misunderstandings of the mystery of the Eucharist

In our catechesis it is helpful to anticipate, and respond to, misunderstandings about the topic we are teaching. In the case of the Mass these misunderstanding often include the following areas:

- the unity of Word and Sacrament
- the Eucharist as a sacrifice
- the Real Presence of Christ
- continuity and change in the Mass.

Unity of Word and Eucharist

The Mass is in two main parts, the Liturgy of the Word and the Liturgy of the Eucharist. Both the Scriptures and the Body of Christ are given to us to bring us into communion with God. The Scriptures communicate the divine life to us as the Body and Blood of Christ.

In the past, the Liturgy of the Eucharist has tended to be so highly regarded that the Liturgy of the Word has sometimes been undervalued. The Church has, in fact, always venerated the divine Scriptures: think of the jewelled Gospel books and the solemn processions of the Gospel book. By comparison, how often do people read from missalettes, photocopies or bits of paper today, and show little reverence for the lectern? Nonetheless, a new appreciation of the Liturgy of the Word was a fruit of the Second Vatican Council, and it is a point upon which we can focus in our catechesis.

4 *How do we show respect for the lectern, the readings and the Gospel?*

The Liturgy of the Word and the Liturgy of the Eucharist are intimately related.

The Sacrifice of the Mass

The Mass is not just a 'Church service', an act of worship devised by the Church. It is, first and foremost, a Sacred Mystery given to us by Christ. In the Mass the sacrifice that Jesus completed on Calvary becomes present for us as we re-enact the events of the Last Supper. In the Mass the table of the Last Supper becomes an altar for Christ's sacrifice. Jesus in the Last Supper offers himself in sacrifice 'so that sins may be forgiven'. He is the lamb of sacrifice 'who takes away the sins of the world'. At the heart of this sacrifice is love.

The Mass, then, is a sacrifice because it makes present the sacrifice of the Cross, applying the redemptive fruits of that sacrifice to those present. In the Eucharistic sacrifice the priest, at the altar, stands in the place of Christ, the great High Priest: he acts 'in the person of Christ'. In the Mass we are led to the heart of the mystery through appreciating the sacrificial nature of what is happening.

The sacrifice of the Cross is made present for us at Mass.

The Real Presence of Christ

At the heart of the Eucharistic prayer of the Mass are the words of Jesus at the Last Supper transforming the bread and wine into his own body and blood. 'This is my Body... This is the Cup of my Blood'. The Catholic Faith has always held that at the Consecration the bread and wine become Christ's Body and Blood so that only the appearances of bread and wine remain. On the altar, after the consecration, Christ the Lord is present. This is why kneeling in worship and adoration of the Sacred Host is appropriate.

In the Mass, Christ feeds us with himself, not just signs or symbols of himself.

Continuity and Change

The essentials of the Mass cannot change. The liturgy of the Word reflects the Jewish synagogue service that Christ would have attended and the Liturgy of the Eucharist is built around the four key actions of Jesus at the Last Supper: 'taking', 'blessing', 'breaking' and 'giving'.

Blessed Pope John Paul II spoke of the sacred character of the Eucharist in the following way:

> 'Beginning with the Upper Room and Holy Thursday, the celebration of the Eucharist has a long history, a history as long as that of the Church. In the course of this history, the secondary elements have undergone certain changes, but there has been no change in the essence of the "Mysterium" instituted by the Redeemer of the world at the Last Supper'. (*Dominicae cenae* 8)

Given all the changes in the liturgy that many have experienced, it is important to stress the central, unchanging elements. It is also important to highlight the need to respect the use of approved liturgical texts in all sacramental celebrations, since it is not only the local parish that is praying in isolation – every parish prays as part of the 'whole Christ'.

The essentials of the Mass are unchanging.

Summary

In this session we have looked at:

- **The meaning of 'mystery'.**
- **The mystery of the Eucharist at the centre of the faith.**
- **How to foster an awareness of the mystery in our catechesis.**
- **Overcoming misunderstandings of the Eucharist.**

Further Reading

- CCC 1076-1109: the Holy Trinity at work in the Eucharist and in the liturgy in general.
- CCC 1145-1162: the importance of signs and symbols for revealing the mystery to us in the liturgy.
- CCC 1179-1186; SC 7, 122-127: the symbolism connected with some of the furnishings in a church.
- CCC 1356-1390: the doctrines of the Eucharistic Sacrifice, the Real Presence and Holy Communion.
- Second Vatican Council: *Dei Verbum* 21: on the veneration due to the one 'table' of the Word of God and Body of Christ.

Glossary on the mystery of the Eucharist

Infinite: *without limits. God is infinite. We are the opposite, 'finite', limited.*

Dominicae cenae: *the Apostolic Letter issued by Blessed Pope John Paul II on the Mystery and Worship of the Eucharist in 1980.*

Sacrament: *an outward and visible sign of an inward and invisible grace, instituted by Christ for our salvation.*

Closing Prayer

*Lord Jesus Christ,
You gave us the Eucharist as the memorial of your suffering and death. May our worship of this Sacrament of your Body and Blood, help us to experience the salvation won for us, and the peace of the kingdom where you live with the Father and the Holy Spirit, One God, for ever and ever. Amen.*

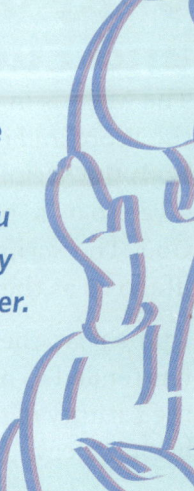

Leading Session 10: What can we do?

Preparation
- Read through session 10 carefully yourself together with these notes before the session. Think about which sections you will ask participants to read.
- Practise the pronunciation of Latin-based words if you are not sure.
- Check particularly that you understand the activities.
- Photocopy a sufficient number of the handout for this session
- Bring to the session: pens, pencils, some paper, a copy of a Bible, a missal and a copy of the Catechism.
- Prepare the room to provide a prayerful and welcoming atmosphere. Get refreshments ready.

At the session
Have the title read out, followed by the sentence from Scripture, and then lead the prayer or ask someone to lead the group into the prayer.

Read out the introductory paragraph or summarise it in your own words to introduce the session.

Stop at the numbered dots

❶ When is it difficult to remain faithful to God in our teaching? There will be a range of suggestions and, in general they will all be valid. To lead people into thinking about it you might start them off with any of the following:

- When I am distracted - such as in the Children's Liturgy by a naughty child
- When I just want to keep the children quiet
- When I find it difficult to agree with, or understand, what the Church teaches on an issue
- When I don't pray enough to 'keep in touch' with God
- When I do not agree with what someone else has said
- When I am feeling downhearted

How do we manage it? Wait for people's own responses, but a few suggestions to get people started could include:

- When distracted, to try and remind myself to return to the point of everything
- When following a less important principle, to try and return to handing on faith
- When finding it difficult to agree with the Church, to resolve to find out more about the Church's reasons for saying what she does
- When disliking or disagreeing, to try to remain 'in Christ', which is to remain 'in charity' to one another
- When feeling downhearted, to remind myself that God is at work at all times and in all things

❷ How does Christ reveal God to us and us to ourselves?

In **Matthew 9:20-22** we have Christ revealing the mercy and compassion of the Father towards the woman as he heals her. Christ's words are words of hope and of encouragement to faith. In the episode he reveals us to ourselves as people needing healing, especially from our lack of faith. He reveals us as people who can be made whole in relation to him.

In **Matthew 14:22-33**, Christ reveals the majesty of divinity to us, he reveals the Lord who has complete authority over creation. He reveals us to ourselves in our weakness and fear, but capable of acts of trust and courage, and of finding true life through worship of the Lord.

❸ What arises from this activity will obviously be specific to the particular group. The activity is built into the session to stimulate discussion of two kinds – praiseworthy recognition of elements that are present in parish activities and discussion of how some catechetical sessions might be able to add new elements.

Read the *summary* and finish with the *final prayer*.

Session 10 — Handout 1

Christ reveals God to us and us to ourselves

"Then suddenly from behind him came a woman, who had been suffering from a haemorrhage for twelve years, and she touched the fringe of his cloak, for she was thinking, 'If only I can touch his cloak I shall be saved.' Jesus turned round and saw her; and he said to her, 'Courage, my daughter, your faith has saved you.' And from that moment the woman was saved."

Matthew 9:20-22

"And at once he made the disciples get into the boat and go on ahead to the other side while he sent the crowds away. After sending the crowds away he went up into the hills by himself to pray. When evening came, he was there alone, while the boat, by now some furlongs from land, was hard pressed by rough waves, for there was a head-wind. In the fourth watch of the night he came towards them, walking on the sea, and when the disciples saw him walking on the sea they were terrified. 'It is a ghost,' they said, and cried out in fear. But at once Jesus called out to them, saying 'Courage! It is I! Do not be afraid.' It was Peter who answered. 'Lord,' he said, if it is you, tell me to come across the water.' Jesus said, 'Come.' Then Peter got out of the boat and started walking towards Jesus across the water, but then noticing the wind, he took fright and began to sink. 'Lord,' he cried, save me!' Jesus put out his hand at once and held him. 'You have so little faith,' he said, 'why did you doubt?' And as they got into the boat the wind dropped. The men in the boat bowed down before him and said, 'Truly, you are the Son of God.'"

Matthew 14:22-23

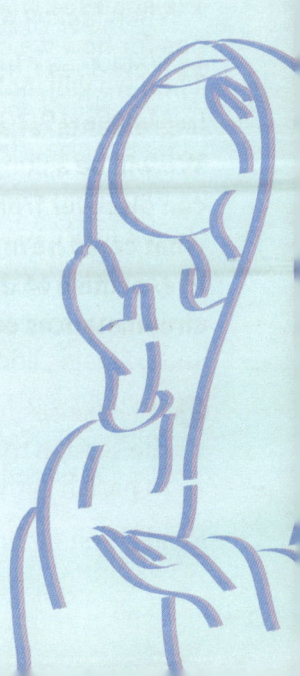

Session 10

'What can we do?'

'Do whatever he tells you' (Jn 2:5)

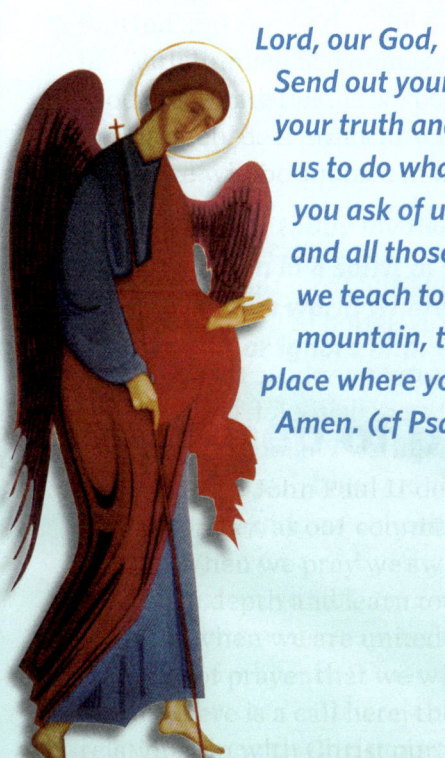

*Lord, our God,
Send out your light and your truth and guide us to do whatever you ask of us. Lead us and all those whom we teach to your holy mountain, to the place where you dwell.
Amen. (cf Psalm 43:3)*

In this session we are going to focus upon God's way of teaching, a way which has been revealed in Christ. We shall see what implications this has for how we can catechise or help. Then we will look at the structure and 'ingredients' of a catechetical session. We will be asking what guidance we can discover from the Church about what could be in a catechetical session, irrespective of the subject, age group or circumstances of those we are teaching.

A double faithfulness

In our catechetical work we practise a double faithfulness:
- to God and the message he has given
- to the human person, the hearer who is to receive the message.

We must hand on the full message we have been given, without any dilution or mutilation. John Paul II says: 'the person who becomes a disciple of Christ has the right to receive "the word of faith" not in mutilated, falsified or diminished form but whole and entire, in all its rigour and vigour.' (CT 30)

We must hand on the full, undiluted message of Christ in a manner which is appropriate for the particular people to whom we are speaking. The *General Directory for Catechesis* tells us that good catechesis consists in that which enables 'the communication of the whole word of God in the concrete existence of people' (GDC 146).

It is important to remember that human differences should not affect the essential content to be transmitted but only the manner of teaching or transmitting. For example, the reality of the Eucharist is the same for children and for adults, for all nationalities and races, for rich and for poor. *How* one teaches about the Eucharist needs to be different for different audiences, the essence of the teaching must be the same.

Blessed Pope John Paul II sums up these points when he speaks about the methods we use to communicate the faith, 'the method chosen must ultimately be referred to a law that is fundamental for the whole of the Church's life: the law of fidelity to God and of fidelity to man in a single loving attitude' (CT55).

In catechesis we practise a double fidelity: to God and to the human person.

① Think about the question of fidelity to God in our teaching. When is this difficult? How do we manage it?

The Pedagogy of God

God has his own way of teaching, a way that is faithful to who he is and to the human person. God practises the double faithfulness about which we have been speaking. The Church calls God's own teaching methods 'the pedagogy of God'.

'Pedagogy' means 'way of teaching' and God has his own ways of teaching about himself, of reaching and revealing himself to people's hearts and minds. The fullest expression of God's pedagogy is found in the sending of the Son.

God's method of teaching about himself, then, is *personal*. He does not choose firstly a written text, or an object, but a *person* for the fullest revelation of himself to us. This is God's pedagogy and it has implications for us as catechisers, for we can imitate God in his methods. We can follow God's ways, which are revealed in Christ.

The *General Directory for Catechesis* helps us to see what this entails, and especially the **focus upon conversion** in Christ's teaching.

Jesus taught to bring about conversion and so in our catechesis we need to bear the person's salvation in mind and not be content merely with communicating facts or hoping to give a good experience. The whole world needs to 'hear the summons to salvation, so that through hearing it may believe, through belief it may hope, through hope it may come to love' (DV 1). The attitude of the catechist, therefore, should mirror that of Christ who received people 'as persons loved and sought out by God' (GDC 140).

We cannot escape this continual reference in the Church's documents to catechesis being for the sake of conversion. This does not mean that any pressure for conversion need come from us; God will speak to the person's conscience. But our manner of speaking, our attitudes and what we say can help prepare a person to welcome the action of the Holy Spirit in his or her life. And so we need to consider the way we think, act and speak, the way we encourage, the way we relate what we teach to happiness, to courage, to suffering, to decision making and to joy.

God has a unique way of teaching which we can follow.

Christ and our human experience

We have seen that God the Father teaches by sending his Son, Jesus. In the mystery of the Incarnation God united himself to every human person who has ever existed or will exist – to every one of us – by taking on human nature and living a fully human life.

By doing this, God the Son has not only revealed who *God* is to us, he has also revealed who we are, what a fully human life is. Here is a wonderful quotation from the Second Vatican Council explaining this, a quotation that has been repeated more than any other from the Council by Blessed Pope John Paul II:

> 'In reality it is only in the mystery of the Word made flesh that the mystery of man truly becomes clear' (GS22).

There has been considerable debate about whether one should begin one's sessions from 'God's side', proclaiming and explaining the truths of Revelation contained in the deposit of faith, or whether one should begin from our own experiences, with what is familiar to us and from there try to understand God's revelation in Christ.

The Church asks us not to oppose these two – doctrine and experience (cf. CT22) – but to **focus upon Christ**. We focus upon Christ because he is both fully God and fully man. Through his life, his teaching and his death and Resurrection, Jesus reveals God to us and us to ourselves. It is by coming to know about Jesus that we understand the Church's doctrine about God, and we can look to Jesus also to show us what human life is about. Rather than draw from our own limited experiences to learn about Christ, we can turn to Christ who wants to give us an experience of himself and his Redemption.

❷ **Let us consider two examples from the Gospels: Matthew 9:20-22 and 14:22-33. How does Christ reveal God to us and us to ourselves?**

We can make sure our catechesis is centred on Christ who reveals God to us and us to ourselves.

Basic structure for a catechetical session

In *Echoes*, we have considered a number of attitudes and fundamental methodological principles. Now let us draw together what we have examined here and in previous sessions to see what guidance this gives for the structure and content of catechetical sessions.

What does a catechetical session need to contain in order to be faithful to God and to the person and to follow God's own pedagogy which is re-vealed in Christ? Here are some points to consider:

- **Catechesis is above all the work of the Trinity** It makes sense, therefore, always to start with a way of acknowledging the presence of the Trinity. This could be a time of quiet, or of prayer, or it could mean opening with a hymn or a short meditative reading from Scripture.

- **Catechesis hands on what God has chosen to reveal of himself and his plan of love.** It makes sense, therefore, to select systematically from the deposit of faith entrusted to the Church. Here we have all that God has revealed of himself and his plan. We turn to Scripture, to the Catechism, to the great Doctors and Councils of the Church and to the writing of the Popes.

- **Catechesis needs to give people knowledge of the story of salvation.** All teaching should be linked into the Story of Salvation in some way. This is the Catholic story which we invite our hearers to understand as their Story, too.

- **Catechesis brings people into communion with Christ.** It makes sense, therefore, to have various activities to help people link their lives and experiences with the life of Jesus so that they can understand how the grace of God in Christ can change our lives, filling us with faith, hope and love.

- **Catechesis always aims at conversion of the person.** God created us out of love, and has revealed his merciful plan to redeem us from sin and death in order to bring us to share in the eternal joy of the Trinity. Our catechesis is therefore always aimed at highlighting God's saving work, offered to us in Christ. Our catechesis will include clear ways to respond to the gracious invitation of God so that his image might be restored in us.

- **Catechesis brings us to the liturgy where we receive Christ and join our lives to him.** It is good to always link our catechesis to the liturgy in some way and conclude our sessions with a form of worship. This might be a simple prayer of thanksgiving for whatever has taken place, acknowledging the work of the Trinity, or the session might lead into Benediction or into a Mass. We invite those whom we are catechising into worship of the One they recognise and claim as their Lord.

So, we can sum up the elements we have been considering as:

- Being rooted in the presence of God
- Communicating the deposit of faith
- Telling the Story
- Relating to Christ
- Seeking Conversion
- Linking to liturgy and worship

These elements can be present in every catechetical session.

All catechetical sessions will contain certain ingredients in order to be faithful to God and to the person.

3 Think of a catechetical session in which you were involved. Which of the elements which we have looked at were included? How might you have included the other elements?

Summary

In this session we have looked at:

- **the double fidelity we are called to practise to God and to the human person.**
- **God's unique way of teaching which we can follow.**
- **the importance of centring our catechesis on Christ who reveals God to us and us to ourselves.**
- **some key components of a catechetical session.**

Further Reading

- On the pedagogy of God: GDC 139-147.
- On doctrine, experience and the centrality of Christ: CCC 425-429 and CT 5-9, 22.

Glossary on Pedagogy

Pedagogy: *way of teaching, especially referring to children. The pedagogy of God, is God's way of teaching us as his own children.*

Methodology: *a system of ways of doing, teaching or studying something.*

Methodological principles: *principles are starting points. Every one has them whether they realise it or not. Typical examples would be 'above all keep them quiet', or 'the main thing is to keep them happy'. These are principles or starting points that guide the methods people choose. The Church asks our starting point to be the double fidelity we looked at.*

Final Prayer

*Our Father,
Who art in Heaven,
Hallowed be thy name.
Thy kingdom come,
Thy will be done,
On earth as it is in heaven.
Give us this day our daily bread
And forgive us our trespasses
As we forgive those who trespass against us.
And lead us not into temptation
But deliver us from evil.
Amen.*

Leading Session 11 – What next?

Preparation
- Read through session 11 carefully yourself, together with these notes, before the session.
- Think about which sections you will ask participants to read. Practise the pronunciation of Latin-based words if you are not sure.
- There are no handouts for this session.
- Bring to the session pens, pencils, some paper, a copy of a Bible, and if possible a copy of *Novo Millennio Ineunte*.
- Prepare the room to provide a prayerful and welcoming atmosphere and get refreshments ready.
- As this is the final session you might think of concluding with a Mass, and some more substantial refreshments. Make it celebratory!
- If you are giving out Certificates this might take place at a further Mass, with a commissioning of those who have followed the sessions.

At the session
Read the title, followed by the sentence from Scripture, and then *pray*.

Then read the introductory paragraph or summarise it in your own words.

Stop at the numbered dots

❶ You may want to pause here for a short time of reflection: what is this passage saying to us about our catechetical ministry? What is it saying about our relationship with the Lord?

❷ You might comment here on the Church placing a new priority on adult learning. As Catholics we are lifelong-learners. Disciple means 'learner'.

You may want to draw attention to the distance-learning courses on the final sheet in their pack. As catechists we keep learning all of the time so that we continually deepen our knowledge of the Lord and of his plan of salvation and can speak of him and his love more and more confidently and effectively. You may want to have already investigated some of the possibilities of courses available which could be promoted in the parish.

One of the issues here is the need to overcome barriers to learning in adults. Many adults carry with them a sense of failure and difficulty from previous educational experiences, and this makes them reluctant to engage in learning, to 'put out into the deep' in this area. There is a need for the healing of memories here and a trust that such barriers can be overcome. Explicitly recognising these points in the group can be very important and a word of encouragement can be given. You may like to make links here with the parable of The Sower. The Word of God could not take root for a number of reasons and these need to be addressed so that the Body of Christ can joyfully and gladly embrace learning about the faith. It is important that this session is seen both as a point of completion and as a renewed invitation to embrace learning about the faith.

❸ This is the question of how we transmit initial proclamation to those who come for catechesis. Remind participants of the way in which the Catechism gives the *kerygma* in its presentation of all topics.

Blessed Pope John Paul II summed up the heart of the Gospel as 'you are saved and loved by God' (*Redemptoris missio*). How is this basic truth, the centre of the Gospel, communicated through the Sacraments of Reconciliation, the Eucharist, Baptism, and Matrimony? How can we make initial proclamation more prominent?

❹ Spend time on the final meditation. It should lead very peacefully into the final prayer. Together these two remind us both of the priority of grace and of the confidence which we can have because God is with us.

Session 11

What next?

'Put out into the deep!' (Lk 5:4)

Lord Jesus, we put our trust in you and step out to you in faith. May we always keep our gaze fixed on you, knowing that you are the Lord of all things, and that in our time of need you will always stretch out your hand to save us and bring us your peace. Amen

In this final session we have a sense of both a finishing and a beginning. We are finishing this short series but we are also looking forward to what needs to be done for Christ and his Church, what needs to be done to make the infinite mercy and love of God real for those around us. The Church says that catechesis is intimately connected to evangelisation. We will look at what this means and at the call to us to be evangelisers, as well as to take our continuing development in faith, hope and love seriously.

We have opened this final session with a quotation from the Gospel of St Luke. Blessed Pope John Paul II, in his Apostolic Letter for the new millennium, *Novo Millennio ineunte* (NMI), uses this phrase to sum up what Christ is asking of his Church. We are to 'put out into the deep'. As we do so, says Blessed Pope John Paul II, we can 'remember the past with gratitude... live the present with enthusiasm and ...look forward to the future with confidence' because 'Jesus Christ is the same yesterday and today and for ever' (Heb 13:8). The Lord is always with us, to the end of time.

❶ Let us read the account of the episode from St Luke from which the quotation comes. (Luke 5:1-11)

The deep of the Good News

What is the deep into which we are to entrust ourselves? The *good news of God* has never-ending depths. God sent his whole Word, plan and desire in his Son, to show and tell mankind, finally and definitively, everything he wanted people to know about himself, about themselves and about ultimate happiness. The Church uses the word evangelisation for the depths and extent of passing on this good news. Are we convinced of this good news ourselves in order to be able to help others to know it?

The document on evangelisation, *Evangelii nuntiandi*, explains to us the content of the good news that we have to offer:

> 'Evangelisation will always contain, as the foundation, the centre and the apex of its whole dynamic power, this explicit declaration: in Jesus Christ who became man, died and rose again from the dead, salvation is offered to every man as the gift of the grace and mercy of God himself.'
> (see Lk 4:22; EN 27)

The Church recognises **three stages of evangelisation** – that is, of discovering and offering to others God's good news:

- The first is called **initial proclamation** – if no one hears the good news very simply they will never know what it is about.
- The second stage is called **catechesis**. Once people have heard the good news and have responded to Christ in faith, they want to learn much more.

(89)

- The third stage is **on-going formation**. This is the desire to go deeper and deeper into the good news because it has been found as the pearl of great price, the only thing that satisfies us to the depths of our being. The Church encourages us to think in terms of a lifelong learning of the Faith.

Jesus Christ and the salvation he brings is the heart of the good news, good news with unfathomable depths about which we can discover more and more.

The deep of the person

Catechesis, then, is a vital part of the great process of evangelization, making God's good news known, loved and lived. A lack of **initial proclamation** which really touches a person deeply hinders the desire for catechesis. Without **catechesis** there is no deepening of the message, no development of life 'in Christ', no growth in understanding of that which matters more to living than anything else. A lack of **on-going formation** hinders adult life because a superficial knowledge of the Faith cannot sustain one in the deep complexities of adult experience.

We need to participate in all three stages of evangelization. We need to do so for the sake of our Christian growth and because God and his plan of love for the world is that which is most rewarding to learn about.

❷ **Each person needs to be evangelized throughout his or her lifetime.**

New evangelisation

For many in the Western world catechesis has taken place without any significant desire for it, or conversion to Christ accompanying it. People know about Jesus but this has not deeply affected their lives. The Holy Father speaks of the need for 'a new evangelisation' for such people:

> 'Frequently, many who come for catechesis truly require genuine conversion. Only by starting with conversion can catechesis, strictly speaking, fulfil its proper task of education in the faith'. (GDC 62; CT 19)

In fact, it cannot be assumed that *initial proclamation, catechesis,* and *ongoing formation* have taken place in that order at all.

It is good to avoid the danger of thinking that a particular 'stage' in evangelisation is complete and finished with, or that the majority of the people in our churches are simply in the process of maturing in faith. This may not be the case at all. There are likely to be significant and important elements missing in most people's journey of faith, and elements in need of reawakening and renewal.

❸ **What implications might there be here for catechesis in your parish?**

In our catechesis we need to bear in mind the need to give initial proclamation as well.

The deep of the world

The opening quotation from the Gospel of St Luke suggests that the apostles are to go deep into *the world* to 'pay out their nets for a catch'. St Luke records Jesus' teaching in the Parable of the Sower (Mk 4:3-8) which explains what the world is like. In this parable Jesus describes the world in terms of different types of soil in which the seed of the Word of God is sown.

> 'Today, Jesus Christ, present in the Church through his Spirit, continues to scatter the Word of the Father ever more widely in the field of the world. The conditions of the soil into which it falls vary greatly.' (GDC 15)

The Parable of the Sower speaks of the hard path, the rocky soil, the choked soil and finally the good, fruitful soil. The world into which we echo the Word of God has the same mix of soils, some receptive and welcoming; some indifferent and some hostile to the seed. In his encyclical letter on catechesis, Blessed Pope John Paul II wrote this about the less promising soils:

> 'Christians today must be formed to live in a world which largely ignores God... To "hold on" in this world, to offer to all a "dialogue of salvation" in which each person feels respected in his or her most basic dignity, the dignity of one who is seeking God, we need a catechesis which trains the young people and adults of our communities to remain clear and consistent in their faith, to affirm serenely their Christian and Catholic identity, to "see Him who is invisible", and to adhere so firmly to the absoluteness of God that they can be witnesses to him in a materialistic civilization that denies Him.' (CT 57)

Whatever the soil, we are still faced with the identical task: to bear witness, simply and clearly, to God as he is revealed by the Lord Jesus Christ. We bring the Good News to all. The *General Directory for Catechesis* asks us to bear the 'field' in mind in a spirit of 'faith and mercy'. We are to look upon the field as God does, with his merciful eyes, longing for the salvation of all.

We can go deep into the world because the world has this depth. We know that every person has been created by God and for God and can find happiness only in a life with him. As St Thomas Aquinas said, 'God alone satisfies'. If we put out our nets in this deep, bearing clear witness to this truth, we will be amazed at our catch.

Echoing Christ today involves bearing witness to him in a spirit of faith and mercy, in a world where many doubt, deny or ignore him.

The deep of prayer

Blessed Pope John Paul II describes the deep as *prayer*, as our communion with Christ. When we pray we swim, as it were, out of our depth and learn to rely on Christ. And it is when we are united to Christ in the deep of prayer that we will make our catch. There is a call here, then, to make our relationship with Christ our priority. Our work in catechesis depends upon this.

Prayer roots us in the truth that our lives and work depend upon Christ.

Go forward in hope!

Blessed Pope John Paul II concludes his Letter for the new millennium by saying that the future opens before the Church 'like a vast ocean upon which we shall venture, relying on the help of Christ. The Son of God, who became incarnate two thousand years ago out of love for humanity, is at work even today: we need discerning eyes to see this, and above all, a generous heart to become the instruments of his work.' (NMI 58)

The men and women around us ask believers not only to 'speak' of Christ, but to 'show' him to them as well. We need to witness to Christ with our lives as well as speak about him. Our witness, however, will be hopelessly inadequate if we ourselves have not first *contemplated his face* in prayer. As our footsteps 'travel the highways of the world', says Blessed Pope John Paul II, we must set our gaze ever more firmly on the face of the Lord. (NMI 16, 58)

The *General Directory for Catechesis* concludes with this reflection: 'May patience and trust abide in the spirituality of the catechist, since it is God himself who sows, gives growth, and brings to fruition the seed of his word, planted in good soil and tended with love.'

The effectiveness of catechesis, says the Directory, is a work of grace, 'is and always will be a gift of God, through the operation of the Spirit of the Father and the Son.' The authors of the Directory remind us of St. Paul who, in his first letter to the Corinthians, confirms this total dependence on grace, the work of God: 'I planted, Apollos watered, but God gave the growth. So neither he who plants, nor he who waters is anything, but only God who gives the growth' (1 Cor 3: 6-7). (see GDC 288-9)

Summary

In this final session we have considered:

- Blessed Pope John Paul II's call to 'put out into the deep'.
- The variety of conditions of the people we meet.
- Being sure that we know in our minds and our hearts what is the 'good news' which we are offering.
- The three stages of deepening the faith and the need for our catechesis to link to initial proclamation and to on-going formation.

Further reading

- For the three stages of evangelisation and their relationship to each other: GDC 60-72.
- For the need to root ourselves in prayer: CCC 2559-2565; NMI 32-34.

Glossary on evangelisation

Evangelisation: *proclaiming the good news of Jesus Christ who has revealed the mystery of God and his plan of love. It comes from two Greek words, 'eu' meaning 'good' and 'angelion' meaning message ('angelos' or 'angel' means messenger).*

Gospel: *'Gospel' comes from two Anglo-Saxon words, 'god' meaning 'good' and 'spell' meaning 'speech' or 'message'. Gospel, then, also means 'good news'. Four evangelists wrote the four Gospels. That is, four messengers of good news wrote four accounts of good news.*

New evangelisation: *where the baptised have lost a living sense of faith, or even no longer consider themselves members of the Church and live a life far removed from Christ and his Gospel. Such situations require a new evangelisation (cf. GDC 586).*

The new situation is the situation of people who may have had to study Christianity, such as in school, but for whom no depth in the message has been grasped and no depth in the person has been reached.

Initial proclamation: *the first proclamation of the Catholic faith, giving the centre and heart of the good news.*

Formation: *the development of the whole person in Christ.*

On-going formation: *a continuing exploration of the fathomless riches of God's revelation.*

Final meditation and prayer

'Indeed we also work, but we are only collaborating with God who works, for his mercy has gone before us. It has gone before us so that we may be healed, and follows us so that once healed, we may be given life; it goes before us so that we may be called, and follows us so that we may be glorified; it goes before us so that we may live devoutly, and follows us so that we may always live with God: for without him we can do nothing.'

(St Augustine of Hippo)

*God our Father,
We praise you that you have made us for yourself. You have given us life that we may come to know you, the fullness of our joy and the end of all our desires. We place your Church under the protection of Mary our Mother, St Joseph, St Michael, the angels and all the saints. As we go forward in hope, continue to fill us with your grace so that we may speak of you and your truth, goodness and beauty, and witness to you with our lives. We ask this in the power of your Spirit and in the name of your Son, who is our Way, our Truth and our Life. Amen.*

COMMENTS AND EVALUATION FORM

I would be very grateful if you would fill in this comments sheet so that I can look at how you have found Echoes, and at the next steps for the parish.

How did you find the content of the sessions?

Too difficult ☐
Challenging but worthwhile ☐
Just about right ☐
Too simple ☐

Do you feel better equipped to hand on the faith to others?

Much better ☐
Yes ☐
I'm not sure ☐
No ☐

Overall, have you benefited from following these sessions?

Very much ☐
Quite a lot ☐
In some ways ☐
Not very much ☐

What did you enjoy most about the sessions?

....
....
....
....
....
....

Was there anything you didn't like? If so, how could this be improved?

....
....
....
....
....
....

Is there anything that you would like to know more about, that we could perhaps consider at another time?

....
....
....
....
....

How do you think you would like to use what you have learned?

....
....
....
....
....

What would you like to do next?

....
....
....
....
....

Any other comments?

....
....
....
....
....

Thanks for filling this in.

God bless!

Notes

Notes

MARYVALE INSTITUTE

Courses for Adult Formation

You can study the Faith at home or lead study groups in the parish using Maryvale's courses in the faith.

Scripture
Study any of the books of the New Testament by following the Maryvale course, New Testament Studies by using Maryvale materials at home. New Testament books are studied over a twelve-week period. You look at the way in which the Church has read and used these inspired texts in the development of her doctrine and in the liturgy. You look at what scholarship says about the texts and learn to pray with them so that reading the Scriptures truly becomes an encounter with the living Lord in the Spirit.

The Catechism of the Catholic Church
Study the definitive presentation of the Catholic faith for our day. This course provides a commentary on each paragraph and section of the Catechism, helping the interested adult to appreciate the teaching contained in this work of the universal Church. The course is divided into 6 twelve-week sections so that it can be followed at a pace which suits lay people with many commitments. It is ideal as a parish or home study course.

New Evangelisation and Ministry
Two year courses in the knowledge and skills for youth ministry, family ministry, parish evangelisation and ministry to the sick can be followed. All of the courses emphasise the importance of a new evangelisation and are placed in the context of Pope John Paul II's vision for the Church in the new millennium.

For all of these, please contact the Director of the relevant course at Maryvale Institute.

Courses for Catechist Formation

Distance-learning programmes in catechist formation are available to enable you to develop your skills and understanding of the Faith.

Certificate in Parish Catechesis
A two-year programme of essential formation, in knowledge, understanding and skills, approved by the Congregation of the Clergy, and used in many dioceses in Europe and Africa for the training of catechists.

B.Divinity (Ecclesial Service)
This degree provides a unique opportunity for formation in theology and the transmission of the Faith. This programme is an award of the Holy See and is validated by the Faculty of Notre Dame in Paris.

MA in Religious Education and Catechesis
A 2-3 year distance-learning programme for the in-depth study of an authentically Catholic approach to religious education and catechesis, enabling mature reflection on the Church's vision for the transmission of the Faith in today's culture.

For all of these, please contact the Director of the relevant course at Maryvale Institute.

Maryvale Institute, Old Oscott Hill, Kingstanding, Birmingham B44 9AG
Tel: 0121 360 8118 · Fax: 0121 366 6786 · Email: enquiries@maryvale.ac.uk · www.maryvale.ac.uk